OVER GWYNEDD

Wings of War
Over Gwynedd

Aviation in Gwynedd during World War II

Roy Sloan

GWASG CARREG GWALCH

ISBN: 0-86381-189-2

Cover design: Anne Lloyd Morris

First published in 1991 by Gwasg Carreg Gwalch,
Capel Garmon, Llanrwst, Gwynedd, Wales, LL26 0RL.

Tel: 0690 710261

Contents

Foreword

I was very pleased to be given the opportunity of writing a foreword to this fascinating and readable book on aviation in Gwynedd in the Second World War. Is is especially appropriate at the 50th Anniversary of the Battle of Britain to be reminded of what people had to put up with all those years ago. Normally, of course, one thinks of those who were killed or injured in the great air battles, but equally a large number of people worked extremely hard to train aircrew, often in difficult surroundings and with little reward or recognition. Many of these men, both trainers and those they trained, are acknowledged in this book. Although there were obviously advantages in being in a relatively safe part of the country, and not subject too much to the rigours of rationing by all accounts, the living conditions were clearly not quite what people take for granted today. It is also sobering to reflect that RAF Valley, which in 1944, for example, had over 2,000 personnel now holds only some 960 servicemen and women, and yet manages to operate a large number of modern and complicated aircraft and trains some 120 pilots every year. I commend this book to anyone with an interest in military history, aviation and the county of Gwynedd.

A J GRIFFIN
Group Captain
Officer Commanding
RAF Valley

Introduction and Acknowledgements

In the field of aviation the momentous period of the second World War brought major changes to Gwynedd and I have attempted in this book to provide an account of these developments. More or less untouched by aviation in any significant form until the outbreak of war, the county had, within the space of two years, seven military airfields under construction.

These were used by the RAF predominantly for aircrew training purposes, although two, Valley and Llanbedr, were bases for operational fighter squadrons during the first years of the war.

Gwynedd was located well away from the concentration of enemy activity in southern Britain and was thus suitable for use as a training area. Bearing in mind this fact, it must be said at the outset that operational flying in this region was limited. Nevertheless, many of the squadrons who flew from Gwynedd's airfields did succeed in intercepting enemy aircraft on a number of occasions. Accounts of all interceptions are given in the relevant parts of the text.

Briefly, the stories told here include, in the main, those of aircrew training (air gunnery, bomb aiming and navigation), target towing, operation of pilotless drones, conversion of American flying boats to meet RAF requirements, the problems of turning a fighter airfield into a transatlantic terminal and flying accidents in the mountains of Snowdonia.

The bulk of my research was carried out in the mid 1980s after I had decided to improve my scanty knowledge of local aviation history. Once I had embarked upon this research, rather haphazardly at first I have to admit, it seemed to gather a momentum of its own and I found myself devoting a great deal of time and effort to exploring the subject in depth. The result is the present volume.

My primary sources of information have been the Air Ministry and RAF files dating from World War II, now deposited in the Public Record Office at Kew, London. The Operations Record Books (ORBs), which are in effect official diaries of events, for the airfields of Gwynedd and their associated units, training schools, squadrons etc. are all to be found here. The PRO is without question a magnificent archive and the amount of material available is vast. It was very gratifying to discover at first hand that the history of individual RAF units had been recorded in so much detail.

Yet for all its excellence the PRO can be just a little bewildering, especially for a novice researcher. I came away feeling disappointed after my first visit, having wasted a great deal of time struggling with volumes of indexes and trying to understand the computerised ordering system for files. This visit had to be written off as a 'learning experience' but subsequently I became more adept at obtaining the files I wanted.

Once, I spent the whole of my summer holidays at the Public Record Office. Whilst all my friends and colleagues seemed to be enjoying themselves on sun-kissed Spanish beaches or Greek Islands I spent a very busy fortnight making copious notes from airfield and squadron ORBs!

Besides the official documents which I consulted I also sought the very different kind of information to be had from individuals. As a result I had the pleasure of meeting and corresponding with many ex-aircrew who have been kind enough to share with me their memories and personal stories. Some have gone to a great deal of trouble to put their recollections into written form and I am most grateful to them for doing so.

In particular I would like to thank J. Shelby-James, Fred Webster, Dennis Knock, W. Curtis and Emrys Edwards for their contributions to the chapters on RAF Mona and Bodorgan. Also W. A. Summers for information on Hunting Aviation and Ted Lane for his account of the time he spent at Hell's Mouth. I did not think I would succeed in locating anyone who had served at this small and obscure airfield but receipt of Mr Lane's letter proved me wrong I am glad to say.

Requests for information on Penrhos and Llandwrog provided a wealth of superb material, mostly personal stories which I found absorbing and highly amusing. I hope the reader will share my view. My thanks go to Les Sidwell, Ian Ryall, R. Morris, Geoffrey Hall, George Gray and Jim Piggott for their graphic and humorous descriptions of life at these two airfields.

For passing on their knowledge of Saunders-Roe Ltd. I am indebted to J. Morris, who served his apprenticeship with the company, and Carl Butterfield, who was part of the design team at Beaumaris. Thanks also to David Shepherd and Charles Taylor for providing so many photographs.

The chapter on Saunders-Roe is based on an unpublished history of the Beaumaris factory written in 1948 by Frank Bridges at the request of Harry Broadsmith, the factory manager. It proved a most invaluable document and one can only acknowledge the debt owed to Harry Broadsmith for his foresight in ensuring that a comprehensive and detailed record of the work done at Beaumaris would be available for posterity. Without it my task would have been infinitely more difficult.

My thanks also to the staff of the Public Record Office, the Imperial War Museum, RAF Museum, the library staff of the Royal Aeronautical Society, Tomos Roberts, archivist at the University College of North Wales, Bangor, and the staff of Gwynedd Archives.

I am most grateful also to Thomas Parry, Eric Hughes and Denis Ellis for their memories and amusing anecdotes. To Dave Smith, that most interesting of aviation writers, I extend my thanks for all his help and also Charlie Chester, Bert Pudney, Evan Jones, Michael Bayley Hughes, Dennis Pritchard, Dafydd Roberts, Arthur Evans and Bob Roberts.

I have attempted to make the narrative as factually accurate and detailed as possible and also to enliven it at every opportunity by the use of anecdotes and contemporary eye-witness accounts of events. By this method of leavening the dough, so to speak, I hope that I have presented the reader not only with a factual account of wartime aviation in Gwynedd but one that is also entertaining.

Roy Sloan
Brynsiencyn
May 1991

Chapter 1

The Air War comes to Gwynedd

The Second World War brought aviation to Gwynedd on a scale hitherto undreamt of, far surpassing the relatively limited operations of World War I. So rapid and so overwhelmingly urgent was development that it can only be described as explosive. Where previously there had been no activity worth recording suddenly the skies were full of aircraft of many different types ranging from sleek Spitfires to lumbering, obsolete Whitleys, and within a short space of time there were seven new airfields within the boundaries of the county.

These developments were part of the enormous wartime expansion of the RAF. In order to sustain its operational capabilities the service had to embark upon a huge aircrew training programme and many new airfields were required to meet the needs of training schemes. As a matter of policy, navigation and air gunnery training schools were to be located in north western Britain, which was regarded as 'safe' and sufficiently far away from operational areas for training to take place.

Thus the county of Gwynedd came under the close scrutiny of Air Ministry surveyors looking for potential sites. One fact was immediately apparent — the hilly and mountainous nature of the region, containing the highest mountains of England and Wales meant that only the coastal areas and the island of Anglesey could be considered. Unsuitable topography, alone, was enough to rule out airfield development comparable to that seen in East Anglia, for instance.

Nevertheless, despite the general shortcomings of the region, as already mentioned, seven military airfields were built during the early years of the war to operate alongside RAF Penrhos, which had been training air gunners and bomb aimers since 1936.

Three sites were selected in Anglesey — Mona, the old World War I RNAS airship landing ground, Bodorgan, an isolated spot on the island's south west coast and thirdly Tywyn Trewan, seven miles to the north, near the village of Rhosneigr. This latter site became RAF Valley, the most important airfield in the county. A few other sites were looked at, particularly on the north side of the island but they were considered too expensive to develop.

In Caernarfonshire, a small flat peninsula at the southern end of the Menai Straits near Llandwrog provided a suitable site whilst an almost identical type of peninsula sandwiched between mountain and sea at Llanbedr gave the RAF its sixth airfield. The seventh was Hell's Mouth, which already existed as a firing range for Penrhos, and the eight was at Tywyn near the county's southern extremity.

Mona and Llandwrog provided training for aircrew such as navigators, bombers, air gunners, using a variety of aircraft types, many of which were obsolete. Bodorgan and Tywyn, later Llanbedr also, were used as bases for rather unglamorous army co-operation units, towing targets for artillery practice. Hell's Mouth was designed to be a Relief Landing Ground for Penrhos and a general emergency landing ground, but in practice saw very little use during its life. Valley first operated as a fighter station providing defence cover for Liverpool and the Mersey approaches, with Llanbedr under its control as a forward airfield for day operations against enemy raiders in the local sea areas. As the war progressed however, Valley's role changed drastically from that of fighter station to transatlantic terminal. This change occurred when America began to send large numbers of heavy and medium bombers to Britain, from July 1943 onwards. Thousands of these aircraft arrived at Valley en-route to operational bases in England. Following the defeat of Germany in 1945 most returned to the USA, again via Valley.

The other airfields and their associated training schools continued throughout the war with very little change in their roles. The history of wartime aviation in Gwynedd is, essentially, that of the eight airfields and it is their story which forms the major part of the present volume.

But not all aviation developments were initiated by the RAF and Air Ministry however. Two civilian manufacturers, Saunders-Roe and Hunting Aviation, were forced by enemy activity in the south of England to look for other locations less vulnerable to attack and by various means found themselves in Gwynedd.

Saunders-Roe established a flying boat base at Beaumaris, which became a centre for the conversion of American built Catalina flying boats to meet British operational standards, whilst Hunting Aviation took over part of the vast Dinorwig slate quarry near Llanberis and used it to manufacture a variety of aircraft components. The story of these firms contribution to the war effort is related in two penultimate chapters.

The final chapter is devoted to another, and notable, aspect of aviation in wartime Gwynedd, namely the large number of flying accidents which occurred in the mountains of Snowdonia. The region, and North Wales in general, was relatively free of enemy activity and so the RAF's training schools and OTUs, in addition to the locally based units, used the area extensively to carry out air exercises. Problems arose when inexperienced aircrew got into difficulties, either of their own making, such as navigational errors, or as a result of technical malfunction, and then had to deal with these problems when flying over high ground, with its ever present dangers. It was very often a fatal combination and Snowdonia became something of a trap into which many aircraft unwittingly wandered, never to escape. During the period 1940 to 1945 some two hundred aircrew lost their lives and many were injured as a result of these high ground crashes. It is a sombre but nevertheless strangely fascinating subject of great interest to both aviation enthusiast and layman alike.

Although the vast majority of aircraft in the skies of Gwynedd were British or Allied a fair number of German aircraft were also to be seen, but only during the early years of the war. They were either taking part in bombing raids on Liverpool and Merseyside or attacking local shipping, dropping mines in sea lanes and harbour entrances or making reconnaisance flights.

Operating from bases in north west France, after the fall of that country in 1940, the Germans reached their targets by taking a route across the English Channel and south west England to St. George's Channel then heading north across Cardigan Bay before turning east over the Irish Sea and following a line roughly parallel to the North Wales coast.

Although the radio navigational aid "Knickebein" was available to bombers flying directly to their targets, aircraft that took the more circuitous but safer route via North Wales had to use less precise methods of navigating. A number of identifiable landmarks existed to help, such as the Great Orme for instance, but on at least one occasion a little extra local assistance was given, according to an intriguing and interesting story told by the well known broadcaster and comedian Charlie Chester. At the time, he was serving with the Royal Irish Fusiliers and was billeted at Maesgeirchen, near Bangor. He relates what happened one evening:

> "Bangor was nothing but a dark void in the hollow below, all blacked out as I looked down from my observation point, when suddenly I saw a pinpoint of light flashing what appeared to be Morse Code signals. I couldn't read Morse but with the stub of a pencil I wrote down on the back of a matchbox the series of dots and dashes being flashed."

> "Then I flew down to the Officer's Mess, to our unit's Intelligence Officer, who was eating his dinner. He was annoyed at being disturbed and said sharply, "What do you want?" I told him about the flashing light and he made me tap the message out with a pencil, reading it from the matchbox; —·, ·——, ··—.

> "He said it was three letters repeated, NWU, NWU, NWU.

"At first he was puzzled by it, but after I had tapped out the message many times over he suddenly shouted, "Good God, it's North Wales University!" I remember the time clearly — thirteen minutes past seven and there were aircraft overhead, German bombers on their way to bomb Liverpool. A night compass was trained on the spot where the light was flashing and I heard later that two men had been apprehended. That was the start of my promotion!"

Gwynedd itself offered few targets and no serious or sustained attacks took place. Holyhead, possibly, was the only exception, receiving the attentions of the Luftwaffe on a number of occasions. Many other parts of Anglesey and Caernarfonshire had bombs dropped on them but only from stragglers or those who failed to find their main target, Liverpool, and then jettisoned their bombs more or less anywhere. Some damage to property resulted, at Maesgeirchen for instance, and some loss of life, but the randomness of this bombing made it totally ineffective.

Other targets included ships in the Irish Sea. The SS *Orford* for example, which was attacked by a Focke Wulf 200 Condor off the coast of Anglesey on 20th August 1940. Later this aircraft was intercepted by fighters from No.10 Group and crashed in the Irish Republic. Another ship was the *Lucellum*, loaded with a cargo of petrol and kerosene, which was bombed near Anglesey on 19th December 1941. The *Lucellum* was eventually salvaged and towed into Holyhead. On 18th January 1941 the *Iris* was strafed by an enemy aircraft off Bardsey Island, seriously wounding the chief engineer. Generally, however, raids against shipping were on a small scale.

Of the airfields, Penrhos was singled out and attacked on five occasions resulting in loss of life plus considerable damage to aircraft and buildings. Llandwrog was also attacked but only once, when a solitary JU88, probably on an anti-shipping raid and flying in bad weather, happened to come across the airfield and took the opportunity of firing at this tempting and unexpected target. Damage was minimal.

As far as the opportunity for fighter squadrons to engage enemy aircraft in combat was concerned, it must be said that only infrequently did the situation arise in this sector which, indeed, because of its rear position, provided a semi-rest for squadrons posted from more active areas. The lack of enemy activity, oft lamented in operations record books, meant that squadrons had to be content with nothing more than routine patrols and exercises which tended to lead to low morale. Few squadron commanders expressed regret on departure.

Yet one should not imagine the sector was totally inactive. Despite the frustration of lengthy periods without interceptions, which was the lot of most pilots, a few did succeed in shooting down German aircraft.

One of the first aerial combats in North Wales took place on the geographical edges of Gwynedd, when, on 7th September 1940 a JU88 flew over the region heading towards Liverpool. It was on a reconnaisance mission but never managed to complete its task. Flying over Hoylake at a height of 20,000 feet the JU88 was seen by the local ROC post and the aircraft was then chased by Spitfires of No.7 OTU Hawarden though none of the pilots were pupils! During this period the north west had no fighter defence to speak of and an unofficial Battle Flight of Spitfires, kept permanently armed, had come into being at Hawarden. On this particular day in September, Sergeant L.S. Pilkington, DFM, an instructor with 7 OTU and also an experienced fighter pilot, was flying one of the armed Spitfires on exercises with a pupil when a message regarding the JU88 was passed to him. The pupil was immediately sent back to base and Sergeant Pilkington set off in pursuit of the enemy aircraft.

Soon he was joined in the chase by another 7 OTU pilot, Wing Commander I. R. Jones, a World War I veteran who though well past the age limit for flying had, nevertheless, managed to pull enough strings to get himself posted to 7 OTU as an instructor. He was delighted to be in the air, 'having a go' at the enemy once again.

But it was Sergeant Pilkington who made the successful interception. In his report he wrote:

> "The twin engined machine was going towards Liverpool, into the sun. I turned, and as soon as he saw me he too turned towards Rhyl, heading inland. I opened up to full throttle and gave the machine, not yet identified, two warning shells — it then returned my fire and did a sharp turn to the right. As it did so I saw the black cross on its fuselage. As I gave it another burst at 400-450 yards range, the JU88 took evasive action, turning right and left, diving and trying to get me into its slipstream."

> "I gave it another burst and it started to lose height. I chased it down to 5,000 feet and got in another burst at close range, 100-150 yards. The last I saw of the machine it was going steeply downwards into thick cloud at 4,000 feet over the mountains, the port engine streaming glycol."

The stricken JU88, piloted by Leutnant Erick Böhle, had escaped from its pursuer by entering cloud but the safety thus gained was illusory only. An equally great danger was presented by the proximity of high ground. When the aircraft, flying on one engine and with control impaired, emerged into clear air below the cloud layer Lt.Böhle found himself in a valley surrounded by mountain slopes rising into the cloud. It was a trap from which the crippled bomber could not hope to escape.

There was no other course of action left open to the pilot except to make a forced landing if he and his crew were not to be killed. Luckily, the valley sides were gently sloping and free from obstruction by large boulders and rocks. The valley was, in fact, the Clywedog, in southern Merioneth. A successful landing was made and the crew survived though all suffered injury of one kind or another.

Lt.Böhle himself was the least injured, with a few broken ribs. Afraid of an explosion or fire he ordered his crew to leave the aircraft as quickly as possible but none could do so because of their injuries. So Lt.Böhle pulled them out of the wreckage one by one and left them a safe distance away before heading downwards to seek assistance. He eventually reached a hill farm from where he was able to summon help for his injured comrades.

They were quickly located by rescuers and taken to the farm, using an old gate as an improvised stretcher! From there they were taken to hospital and eventual incarceration as prisoners of war.

A few weeks later, on the 18th, Hawarden's Spitfires were lucky enough to be in action again when they intercepted a formation of Dorniers flying along the coast towards Liverpool, sending one crashing into the sea and damaging another.

Then on 21st September Pilot Officer D. Adams, flying a Spitfire of 611 Squadron, Tern Hill, attacked a Dornier 17 over Denbighshire. After a long chase he succeeded in shooting it down near Trawsfynydd and within minutes of the crash hundreds of soldiers from a nearby Royal Artillery camp were on the scene. Three of the crew survived and were taken prisoner but a fourth man died. He was 26 year old Unteroffizier Gustav Pelzer, who was buried at Pwllheli with full military honours. In 1965, like all German war dead, his remains were re-interred at the German military cemetery, Cannock Chase, Staffordshire.

Gwynedd had a total of eighteen German graves within its boundaries — ten at Pwllheli, six at Holyhead and two at Tywyn.

The next interception by 611 Squadron took place during the evening of 11th October 1940 when a flight of six Spitfires took off from Tern Hill to patrol North Wales. Whilst flying over Anglesey at 17,000 feet they saw enemy aircraft 3,000 feet below, coming in from the south west. Upon closer inspection the intruders turned out to be three Dornier DO17s, forming part of a 20 strong force of aircraft on their way to bomb Liverpool.

As the Spitfires prepared to attack, one developed engine trouble and was forced to withdraw, later landing safely at Sealand. The other five continued to close upon their target but first to open fire was one of the Dornier's gunners. This alerted the other two bombers who were seemingly unaware of the danger. As a result the formation broke up, with one aircraft heading out to sea and the others turning inland.

Two Spitfires pursued the lone Dornier and eventually shot it down in the sea between Carmel Head and the Skerries. One of the Spitfires was damaged in the encounter, resulting in some loss of aileron control but the pilot made a successful emergency landing at Sealand. Of the German crew one drowned after his parachute harness was caught up in the sinking aircraft, but three men survived, to be picked up later by a trawler and handed over to the authorities at Holyhead. Their uniforms were taken from them and on the following day were put on display in a local shop. A charge was made for viewing, the proceeds going to the local "Spitfire Fund".

Meanwhile, the other two Dorniers were being pursued over Caernarfonshire. One was shot down in the sea off Abersoch, with no survivors, and the other had its starboard engine and bomb bay set on fire. This aircraft was seen in an apparently terminal dive over the Capel Curig area. Two of the crew baled out, one landing safely near Deiniolen but the other man, Unteroffizier Heinz Johannsen, struck the aircraft's tailplane and was killed. His body was later found on the mountainside between Llanberis and Bethesda.

Back in the seemingly doomed Dornier the pilot, Leutnant Kipfmuller, found to his surprise that both fires had been blown out. He managed to regain control and with help from the remaining crew member, Oberleutnant Heine, flew on one engine and without a canopy back to base at Brest in France.

On 31st May 1941 another German aircraft, thought to be a Heinkel, crashed in the sea off Porthdinllaen. Its crew were seen to bale out and Porthdinllaen lifeboat carried out a search but could not find any survivors. Twenty four hours later a JU88 crashed offshore near Barmouth. Again there were no survivors. Some weeks later the bodies of two crew members were washed up on the beach and were subsequently buried at Tywyn.

The interceptions so far described took place during the early days of the war before fighter cover had been extended to Gwynedd. When Valley and Llanbedr came into operation, day and night fighter squadrons provided forward defence for Liverpool and combats that occurred subsequently are described in the chapters dealing with individual airfields.

Another aspect of the war's early days worth mentioning briefly, was the presence of Tiger and Hornet Moths from No.3 Coastal Patrol Flight, Hooton Park, who, between January and May 1940, regularly patrolled the coast of North Wales and Anglesey, in similar fashion to World War I patrols, keeping a watch for enemy submarines although none were ever seen. From June to July 1940 Lysanders of 13 Squadron at Speke maintained these patrols.

On a lighter note, Gwynedd provided good sport for those pilots who wished to indulge in the hazardous activity of flying underneath bridges. The principal attraction was the famous Menai suspension bridge connecting Anglesey to the mainland. It was not at all unusual for local residents to see aircraft from the smallest to the largest flying under this bridge.

One staff pilot from Mona readily admits that he used to relieve the boredom of routine training flights in his Anson by regularly flying under the Menai Bridge, and the Britannia railway bridge, just one mile away, much to the surprise of his unsuspecting pupils!

The Conwy bridge was another under which aircraft flew and there is also a report of a Polish pilot who flew his Spitfire under the railway bridge which crosses the Mawddach estuary near Barmouth. This bridge is very different from the others, presenting a much smaller 'target' with its low height and narrow spans. With no margin for error the Spitfire's pilot must have been either extremely skilled or very lucky.

All such flights were unauthorised of course but probably the most memorable of all these events was officially authorised. It took place during the spring of 1942 when more than twelve Lancasters of 44 Squadron, led by Squadron Leader J. D. Nettleton, flew under the Menai Bridge. They were practising for a low level daylight raid on the M.A.N. diesel works at Augsberg. The raid took place on 17th April but of the dozen aircraft that took part only five returned, whilst Squadron Leader Nettleton was awarded the V.C. for his bravery and courage during the raid.

One observer of 44 Squadron's spectacular flight along the Menai Straits was Denis Ellis, a resident of Menai Bridge town. Then a young schoolboy, he was fascinated by aircraft and aviation. His youthfulness and the limitations imposed by being confined to his immediate environs only, have not detracted from an admirable eye-witness account of his observations. He writes:

> "What I remember most was the sheer scale of local flying activity. It was so intense in comparison to what had happened before, and after the war.
>
> "As a keen spotter there was something new for me every day

almost, there always seemed to be aircraft about and I saw many different types. The most common were the ubiquitous Ansons of Llandwrog and Mona — they were everywhere. But I also saw some of the rarer types such as the Blackburn Roc. Most of these aircraft flew low and slow so it was easy to observe them and make a proper identification.

"I remember particularly the Merlin-engined Beaufighters from Valley as the noisiest aircraft that I have ever heard. When they went over conversation was impossible. I used to see many Whitleys also, from Llandwrog, lumbering along slowly with their characteristic nose down attitude. They used to fly with a hatch cover in the fuselage open and I was intrigued at being able to look inside the aircraft when they were overhead.

"I remember, too, the drogue towing aircraft such as the Lysanders and Henleys with the underpart of their fuselages painted yellow."

"I used to go to school at Beaumaris, where Saunders-Roe had their flying boat base and I remember seeing Catalinas moored on the Menai Straits. They had a white/light grey colour scheme and looked very attractive I thought, with a 'modern' look about them. I also remember seeing a Sunderland there, bristling with antennas and aerials strung along the length of the fuselage. Another unusual aircraft I remember seeing was the Spitfire floatplane, which, I gather, spent some time at Beaumaris. I remember standing in the school playing field when this Spitfire came over, did some aerobatics and then disappeared towards Friars which was only a short distance from the school but in between was a small hill which obscured the view.

"Another memory I have comes from 1940 when RAF Valley was being built. Many lorries, heavily laden with stones from Dinmor Quarry at Penmon, used to go through Menai Bridge on their way to Valley where the stones were used to construct the runways. One morning I was in the town square with my friends on our way to school when a procession of these heavily laden lorries came trundling through. When negotiating a sharp right hand turn in the town square one lorry lost a wheel, which continued to roll merrily along the street whilst the lorry collapsed on to its axle, much to the amusement of watching schoolboys and the discomfiture of the driver.

"I did not see any German aircraft except for a Dornier (I think) being chased by a Spitfire but I don't know what happened to them. However, in 1940 I heard plenty of German bombers flying over at night to bomb Liverpool. Their unsynchronised engines gave them a distinctive sound. From our house we had a very good view along the North Wales coast and we often could see quite plainly a reddish glow on the horizon as parts of Liverpool were set on fire by these bombing raids.

"One of my most vivid recollections is of seeing aircraft flying underneath the Menai Bridge. One day I was walking across the bridge with my brother when suddenly a Lockheed Hudson came swooping down from the direction of Llanfair P.G., levelled out and flew underneath the bridge. I remember looking down and catching a glimpse of the crew sitting in the cockpit as they swept beneath us."

"On another occasion I was near the bridge, when to my surprise, I saw a squadron of Lancasters flying underneath it! (These were from 44 Squadron, as previously mentioned). They were flying at a very low height indeed, more or less at wavetop height, and I remember thinking how small they looked. I would have expected a large aircraft such as the Lancaster to have given the impression of enormous size when flying within the confines of the Straits at their narrowest point but strangely this was not the case. They flew in an easterly direction towards Bangor but not all went underneath the bridge, some went over it. As you can imagine, there was a lot of noise and all in all it was a pretty impressive sight."

In fact, Denis Ellis had been witness to many sights, never to be repeated, in this unique period of Gwynedd's aviation history.

Chapter 2

From Sand Dunes to Fighter Station R.A.F. Valley 1940-1943

There existed, in 1940, an area of small coastal sand dunes between the villages of Valley and Rhosneigr in north west Anglescy. These dunes, known locally as Tywyn Trewan (Trewan Sands), also had many small, marshy lakes nearby plus a myriad of creeks and inlets.

A visitor might find it pleasant and attractive enough here but this stretch of the island's coast already had a place in Welsh history as the hunting ground of one of the most infamous bands of thieves ever to be found in Wales - Lladron Crigyll (Robbers of Crigyll). During the eighteenth century and early part of the nineteenth century they plundered shipwrecks on the rocky coast with impunity and a remarkable freedom from prosecution by the law.

Since the far off days of Lladron Crigyll little had changed at Tywyn Trewan but in 1940 developments were to take place that would alter the character of the area for ever. It had been chosen as the site of a new airfield.

This airfield was necessary because RAF planners had realised in 1940 that Fighter Command's defence cover of north west Britain had been inadequate, as no enemy attacks were expected from the west. But enemy aircraft had been attacking Liverpool, for instance, by approaching from the west, usually flying from bases in northern France up St.George's Channel and across the Irish Sea.

Fighter Command H.Q. and No.9 Group (itself newly formed in 1940) agreed that an additional defence sector should be formed to cover the north west. Existing sectors were regarded as being too large to be easily workable and sector stations were too far inland to control aircraft operating over St.George's Channel, where German aircraft were frequently to be found. An airfield would have to be built on the North Wales coast in order to provide a base for fighters intercepting enemy aircraft approaching from the south west, hence the choice of Anglesey as a location for the new airfield. It would also provide protection for shipping in the Irish Sea and become the sector operations centre, that is if the Air Ministry gave approval for the creation of a new sector. The necessary approval was quickly forthcoming.

Construction of RAF Rhosneigr, as it was to be known (though later changed to Valley) began with the process of levelling the sand dunes.

20

However, once the bulldozers had done their work the cover of Marram grass which previously had stabilised the sand was destroyed. This gave rise to a serious problem which plagued both the civil contractor and the RAF for a long time — wind-blown sand.

Seemingly everlasting sea breezes drove sand relentlessly into everything from workmen's lunch boxes to the filters and intakes of engines. Lorries bogged down with such frequency that lengths of steel matting had to be laid in large quantities otherwise work would have come to a halt completely. Eventually, after levelling was finished attempts were made to stabilise the sand by seeding with grass, which proved ineffective because seedlings were blown away along with the sand. A successful solution to this problem was two years, and many unserviceable aero engines, away.

The opening up party which arrived in February 1941 found a widely dispersed airfield on a bleak site, exposed to strong winds from the sea and with very little in the way of comfort or amenity to make life easier for the occupants.

Three runways had been constructed — NW/SE 1,600 yards, N/S 1,300 yards and NE/SW 1,400 yards. Five radar stations were also built in the sector at strategic points to give the widest possible coverage — Castell Mawr, Rhuddlan, South Stack, Nefyn and Pen-y-Bryn (near Aberdaron).

To digress for a moment, this last mentioned station was not ideally situated for its purpose. According to RAE engineers the best site hereabouts was on the top of Enlli Mountain on Bardsey Island. This would have given maximum coverage free from blind spots but the difficulty of getting materials and equipment across the two mile gap of Bardsey Sound was thought too great. Thus one of Wales' most romantically isolated islands was saved from despoilation.

Another mountain which almost had a radar station on its summit was Snowdon. During 1942 it was decided to provide an Atlantic Radar Chain for Coastal Command, as a navigational aid, with the Master Station on Snowdon's summit. But by the time the Air Ministry had torn down the old wooden Summit Hotel, replaced it with a reinforced concrete structure, installed two massive diesel generators and detailed a crew which included an experienced mountaineer, the project was cancelled. This concrete building still stands and is used to provide refreshment for the thousands of tourists who visit the summit every year.

Radar coverage in the sector was supplemented by a GCI (Ground Controlled Interception) station named Trewan Sands which came under Valley's control. This station, and many others like it, used newly developed equipment capable of long distance radar tracking, which could be used to simultaneously track the progress of a hostile raider and an intercepting fighter. By means of R/T intructions from a ground controller the fighter could be placed within 1,000 yards of its target, the pilot then using AI (Airborne Interception) radar to bring him into visual contact. This system was to revolutionise the techniques of night fighting. Its most serious limitation was the inability to control more than one or, at most, two interceptions at a time.

Valley's first fighter control centre was in a most unwarlike building, the Chapel Hall at Caergeiliog, a small village on the A5 road two miles from the airfield. Similarly, the station's first guardroom was in a small traditional whitewashed Welsh cottage. Later of course, more suitable accommodation was provided.

As mentioned previously the new airfield was known as RAF Rhosneigr to begin with, but staff at No.9 Group quickly realised this name was misleading and inappropriate. For instance, airmen found difficulty in locating the airfield, frequently ending up in the village of Rhosneigr itself; the postal address was Valley and the nearest railway station was also Valley. A proposal was put to Fighter Command H.Q. that the name should be changed to RAF Valley as it was short, simple and Anglicised.

However, Fighter Command did not agree and refused to allow the name change but No.9 Group remained convinced, in the face of much resistance, that the change was necessary. Neither side would yield and so something of an impasse was reached. On 12th March 1941 the Air Ministry was requested to give a ruling on the matter. The Ministry deliberated for a long time, much to the annoyance of the staff at No.9 Group who were eager to resolve the question without delay. On 3rd April a decision came: from 5th April the airfield would become, officially, RAF Valley.

To this rather uninviting place came the first fighters on 3rd March — a flight of 312 Squadron's Hurricanes, from Speke. After a short stay they moved to the Isle of Man in mid April to be replaced by Hurricanes of 615 Squadron, officially on a 'semi-rest'.

Not long after, one of 615's pilots, Flight Lieutenant Haywood saw action on 7th May when he was on patrol over the Menai Straits. Flying at a height of 10,000 feet he saw an enemy aircraft only 500 feet above him. He immediately attacked but three seconds after opening fire his guns jammed. Nonetheless, hits were made before the enemy escaped by diving into cloud over Snowdonia.

A week later Sergeants Hamilton and Roberts contacted and engaged a JU88 whilst on convoy patrol ten miles west of Holyhead. Hamilton silenced the rear gunner and after running out of ammunition broke off the attack, by which time his Hurricane was damaged by return fire and he himself had three bullet wounds in his leg. Sergeant Roberts did not fare particularly well either, his port guns were put out of action and the aircraft considerably damaged. The only consolation was that the JU88 suffered damage also. Both Hurricanes landed safely.

The next combat took place on 27th June, when Flight Lieutenant Haywood and Pilot Officer Strickland intercepted a JU88 twenty miles off Holyhead. A few bursts of fire caused the raider to dive out of sight. Bullets were seen to strike the starboard engine and so the aircraft was claimed as 'damaged'.

On 11th July one of the squadron's Hurricanes crashed on Nefyn beach whilst attempting a forced landing following engine failure during an operational sortie. The pilot, 21 year old Pilot Officer Stephens, brought his aircraft down in a steep glide from 18,000 feet and it seemed, at first, the landing was going to be successful but unfortunately the port wing hit a large rock causing the Hurricane to somersault. It came to rest, facing downwards, in shallow water. People rushed to help the pilot, but somewhat to their mystification he was not to be seen, and in fact half an hour elapsed before his body was found.

Whilst trying to escape, Stephens had been pushed by the weight of the Hurricane completely into the soft wet sand, with the edge of the cockpit across his shoulders.

Planks of wood were used in an abortive attempt to right the plane and the cockpit side was ripped open also, but to no avail, there was no sign of the pilot. Eventually, a policeman noticed a hand sticking up from the sand but by then it was far too late to help the unfortunate pilot. Even after being located, Stephens' body still could not be extricated from the wreckage and rescuers were forced to wait until the tide went out an hour later.

Normally, an inquest would have been necessary but the coroner for Caernarfonshire, Mr E. Robyns-Owen, promptly received a note from Valley's Commanding Officer, Wing Commander J. Oliver, stating that Pilot Officer Stephens' death was due to War Operations and that was the end of the matter. Evidently the CO wished to avoid becoming involved in the formality of an inquest when far more pressing problems faced him.

However, the coroner disagreed and was perturbed enough by the situation to write for guidance from the Coroners Society. He received this reply. . ."The RAF tend to read the definition of War Operations in a way all of their own!. . .the Home Office have very little control over what the RAF actually do. When this matter was under discussion about a year ago, the RAF clearly desired (and understandably) to avoid all contact with coroners. . ." This was borne out by the attitude of Llandwrog's CO following the station's most serious accident in October 1941, which is discussed fully in Chapter 5.

Meanwhile at Valley, 615 Squadron had no further interceptions until 26th August when a JU88 flying over Cardigan Bay was attacked by Flying Officer Mouchotte and Sergeant Hamilton of 'B' flight, resulting in damage which forced the JU88 to land near Cork, in Eire. Also in pursuit were members of 'A' flight but they lost contact after investigating another aircraft which to their disappointment turned out to be friendly. This proved to be the squadron's last interception in North Wales.

Early in September news came through that 615 was posted to Manston. In the squadron commander's words this caused, "great excitement and relief that the 'exile' was over" — a telling comment on the unpopularity of quiet sectors amongst the pilots of operational fighter squadrons.

A few days previously, on 28th August 1941, one of the most dramatic and tragic rescue attempts in wartime North Wales took place. The drama began when Botha L6417, flown by a Polish crew from No.4 AOS, ditched in the sea near Rhosneigr after taking off from Valley in bad weather. When the Botha's crew of three emerged after ditching, two men were swept away almost immediately by heavy seas but the third managed to cling to the aircraft.

With gale force winds driving huge waves on to Rhosneigr beach, two seventeen year old boys courageously launched a small dinghy and set out to the rescue. It took them 45 minutes of hard rowing to reach the aircraft, showing excellent seamanship, for ones so young, in keeping the dinghy afloat. However when they turned to go alongside, their boat was caught broadside by a wave and capsized, throwing both into the water. They swam the few yards to the Botha and joined the surviving crew member. He had been slightly injured and was suffering from shock and exposure.

After regaining their breath the boys decided to make for their dinghy as it was now being driven shoreward. They persuaded the Pole to go with them. He was scarcely able to help himself and had to be supported by the two boys as they struggled to keep their heads above water.

In this way they gradually drifted nearer the shore, without actually succeeding in getting into the dinghy, but using it as a support. Eventually they reached a beach defence post to which the Pole clung with all his remaining strength. The boys struck off again for shore, hoping to reach the relative security of another post if they failed to swim to shore.

A group of soldiers, who by then had gathered on Rhosneigr beach, formed a human chain and managed to rescue the youths but sadly they failed to reach the Polish airman in time. Although he was in his own depth he became so exhausted that he lost his grip on the post and was swept away.

These were not the only rescue attempts however. A group of nine men, including the local policeman, P.C. Arthur, a merchant navy officer and seven soldiers put out in a whaler which nearly reached the Botha but then capsized, drowning six of the men.

Yet another boat put out with an airman and a coastguard officer on board. Their boat also capsized after being battered by heavy seas. The coastguard officer was drowned. By then it was a case of rescuing the rescuers and fourteen men, soldiers and airmen, swam out to try and help those struggling for their lives in the water. Four of this group also drowned. Above this tragic scene aircraft flew, dropping life jackets, most of which were rapidly swept away. Besides the crew of the Botha, eleven men were drowned in this most heroic rescue attempt.

The two 17 year olds, John Wood of Chester and Derrick Baynham of Walton-on-Thames, received the George Medal for their remarkable act of courage, plus the RNLI silver medal. In addition they were given monetary reward from the Air Ministry and silver cases from General Sikorsky, the Commander-in-Chief of Polish Forces.

Others that took part also received awards. The RNLI Bronze Medal for gallantry went to Sergeant C. Jackson, Lance Bombardier T. Taylor and Gunner J. W. Parkinson, the three survivors from the capsized whaler. Aircraftsman A. E. Atkinson, survivor of the second boat also received the Bronze Medal.

Seven men who drowned were awarded the Bronze Medal posthumously — 2nd Lt. Peter Whysall, Sergeant Major Alfred Moger, Gunner Clarence Thornton, 2nd Mate (Mercantile Marine) Arthur J. Owen, Police Constable George Arthur, Coastguard Officer Evan Jones and Gunner Reginald Eaton. In addition the Royal Humane Society rewarded those who made rescue attempts by swimming.

But to return to squadron changes at Valley, 615 departed in September 1941 to be replaced by the Hurricanes of 242 Squadron. They became non-operational however in early October to prepare for an overseas posting and left Valley early in December.

These squadrons provided daytime defence cover primarily, but adequate night cover was also necessary. In May 'A' flight of 219 Squadron was detached from Tangmere for this purpose, operating four Beaufighters. They claimed one success, on 1st June, when Squadron Leader Colbeck-Welsh, on patrol over Anglesey shot and crippled a JU88 which eventually crashed in the sea near Aberystwyth. At the end of the month they returned to Tangmere to be replaced by a detachment from 68 Squadron, High Ercall.

The sector was quiet until October, when on the 12th, Pilot Officer Mansfield and his radar operator, Sergeant Janacek, had a bumper time with no less than five contacts, all JU88s. Under the control of GCI Trewan Sands Pilot Officer Mansfield made contact with his first JU88 at 10.00 p.m. whilst flying north over the Irish Sea but the aircraft escaped.

After further vectors (bearings to steer in order to bring the interceptor into contact with an enemy aircraft in the shortest possible time) from Trewan Sands he made contact with a second JU88 thirty minutes later. At a range of 300 feet the Beaufighter opened fire with two short bursts. Flames appeared on the JU88's port side and it dived steeply, disappearing into cloud. Pilot Officer Mansfield claimed this aircraft as 'damaged'.

The next combat was at 11.00 p.m. when Mansfield opened fire at a range of 250 feet but he did not observe any hits. He then had to take avoiding action to prevent a collision, following which the JU88 escaped.

At 11.25 p.m. the fourth contact of that night was made at a height of 12,000 feet. Closing in gradually to firing range Pilot Officer Mansfield kept the JU88 constantly in view silhouetted against the moon before giving two 1½ second bursts which set the aircraft's starboard wing and engine on fire. It then disappeared from view into cloud. Coastguard and ROC observers reported a fire burning on the water at the time of this attack and so the JU88 was claimed as 'destroyed'.

Then, only five minutes later, another JU88 was shot down by Mansfield in almost exactly the same manner. It fell, burning fiercely, into the sea. These interceptions took place in the Skerries area.

The squadron had its next success on the 22nd when Flying Officer Winward, on patrol at 4,000 feet was vectored by Trewan Sands to intercept an enemy aircraft which, on close inspection, turned out to be a JU88. He successfully attacked this aircraft from a range of 250 feet, resulting in a brilliant white flash — probably exploding flares — from the fuselage. Winward watched the blazing aircraft plunge into the sea near Nevin.

Further success came to 68 Squadron on 1st November. At 9.30 p.m. Pilot Officer Shiphard and his radar operator, Sergeant Oxby, were on patrol over Bardsey at 10,000 feet when Trewan Sands gave vectors for an enemy aircraft at 7,000 feet. Shiphard made radar contact and closed in on his quarry ready for the attack.

In his report on the interception he stated, "I made corrections bringing me within 4,000 feet range. I throttled back to 110 knots i.a.s. and 15° flaps. I closed to 2,000 feet then slowly to 1,000 feet and saw a faint silhouette which I identified as a Heinkel HE111. I increased speed to close the range to 400 feet then eased until I was dead astern 10 or 20 feet below the EA", (enemy aircraft).

"I opened fire at 300 feet with a 2 second burst, the EA starboard engine caught fire and then the whole of the interior seemed to catch fire, the aircraft fell steeply to port, spiralling down until it disappeared in cloud at 7,000 feet. Our aircraft was lit up by an explosion beneath the cloud, later we saw the EA burning on the ground".

"After receiving more vectors with no results I landed at Valley at 2305 hours. During the action I had the moon behind me and apparently I was not seen by the EA as there was no evasive action and no return fire. I fired 62 cannon rounds. Weather 5/10 cloud, brilliant moonlight, excellent visibility, EA crashed six miles east of Valley", signed, P/O Shiphard.

The Heinkel had crashed at Bwlch y Fen Bentir farm near Bodffordd, a small village in the centre of Anglesey. The crash broke every window in the farmhouse but the elderly couple who lived there had a lucky escape from injury by flying glass when they came out of the house to investigate the noise a few moments before the actual impact.

A neighbouring cottage, Tan-y-Bwlch, also suffered damage when ceilings collapsed. One of the cottages' occupants that evening still resides in the area and she recalls the shock of the crash. Then a young woman, she was living with her husband and two children at Tan-y-Bwlch. On this particular evening she was doing some housework whilst her husband was working in the garden shed. The children had been playing happily all evening but as bedtime approached they were reluctant to abandon their play. Because it was proving difficult to get them to bed she called her husband, who, in order to frighten the children a little, said, "Go to bed now, there are Germans around tonight". Little did he know how true his words were to become! A short while later the Heinkel crashed.

To this young woman it was a tremendous shock. She was of a very nervous disposition and the incident was deeply disturbing and traumatic for her, especially the sight of mutilated bodies which she had never seen before. Her distress was not improved by the presence of many curious onlookers wandering around hoping to see something of the Heinkel's wreckage. Even now, nearly half a century later, she dislikes recalling the experience and will only talk about it with reluctance.

Shortly after the crash it was discovered the aircraft had a full bomb load (probably destined for Liverpool) giving rise to the danger of unexploded bombs and so the occupants of Bwlch y Fen Bentir and

Tan-y-Bwlch had to leave their homes temporarily. A map of Holyhead was also found in the wreckage of the Heinkel.

None of the four crew survived, and while the pilot's body was never found the three others were identified and given a funeral with full military honours at Holyhead. Like other German war dead, their remains are now in the military cemetery at Cannock, Staffs.

On 25th November, 68 Squadron's commitment ended because another night fighter squadron had, since the summer, been building up to fully operational status ready to take over.

This was 456 (RAAF) Squadron, formed at Valley on 30th June under Squadron Leader C. Oliver. Equipped with Defiants the squadron became operational in September and thereafter night patrols in the Irish Sea were carried out as normal routine although no contact with enemy aircraft took place. During October the squadron re-equipped with Beaufighters, but not without difficulty as the Defiant gunners had to be retrained as 'Observers Radio' so that they could use AI equipment installed in the Beaufighter. The technique of using airborne radar to intercept raiders was fairly new and not easy to master.

In the autumn of 1941, Valley was judged sufficiently important to warrant protection from enemy attack by the use of a decoy airfield. Staff from Colonel Turner's Department (an Air Ministry department set up by one Colonel Turner, an expert in camouflage and deception techniques) visited Anglesey to look for a suitable location, which had to be fairly close to Valley but not too close. They chose Newborough Warren, an area of coastal sand dunes some nine miles south of Valley. Here, in November, they constructed a decoy site, for night use only, consisting of a runway lighting pattern set amidst thirty foot high sand dunes. Decoys of this nature were designated 'Q' sites whilst those intended for daytime use were known as 'K' sites. This latter type often consisted of elaborate and ingenious deceptions.

Four men, a corporal and three airmen, operated the decoy at Newborough Warren from an enlarged Anderson Shelter (which still remains today), under control from Valley. The work was monotonous and routine — switching and testing of lights, clearing windblown sand from lamps and maintenance of generators etc.

One obvious danger, inherent in 'Q' sites, was the possibility of a friendly aircraft mistaking the lights for those of a real airfield and attempting to land. To prevent this happening the lighting pattern, which was of the standard Drem type, had two safeguards, a screened red bar of lights across the dummy runway threshold, visible only from an angle of 30° or less to the runway axis, and secondly, omission of the T used normally to indicate where landing should take place. Any pilot noting these departures from the normal pattern should therefore be aware that he was at a 'Q' site. The lights could also be switched off completely by the site operating crew if an aircraft persisted in landing. However, in times of stress, during an emergency for instance, the need to land as quickly as possible might overide usual vigilance and these safeguards could easily be overlooked by a pilot, with tragic results. This was clearly demonstrated in an accident at Newborough on 8th October 1942.

No.456 Squadron's Beaufighters were engaged on night exercises for which purpose the 'Q' site was lit. At 11.00 p.m. a young Australian pilot, Sergeant R. Scott, reported by R/T that his starboard engine had failed and that he was returning to Valley immediately. He requested also that the floodlight (a powerful light used to illuminate the runway threshold) be turned on. Scott was then flying at a height of 9,000 feet over Anglesey and he had to descend through layers of cloud from 6,000 feet down to 2,000 feet.

When he emerged from the bottom layer of cloud it happened, by chance, that he did so over Newborough and when he saw the 'Q' site lights he mistook them for Valley, wondering why the floodlight was not on as he had requested. Scott then repeated his request for floodlighting (the light had, of course, been switched on at Valley from the time of his first transmission) but as his request seemed to produce no response he must have felt that he could wait no longer and proceeded to land without doing a proper circuit. The aircraft then collided with the top of a sand dune killing both pilot and observer instantly. Flames erupted from the wreckage which the two airmen on duty that night at Newborough attempted to put out with pitifully inadequate hand held extinguishers. Scott's final approach to the flare path had been at an angle of 90° and so he would not have seen the screened bar of red lights.

Tragic though this accident was, there is a story concerning it which contains an element of humour and is perhaps worth repeating here if only to serve as a good example of natural justice following an act of law breaking by a person responsible for upholding the law.

One of the many people who soon gathered at the site of the Beaufighter's crash was a policeman, whose identity it is better not to disclose but simply to call P.C. 'X'. Whilst investigating the wreckage he found one of the Beaufighter's wing tanks some distance away from the main wreckage. It was relatively undamaged and still had fuel in it. P.C. 'X' decided to steal the fuel tank and in the confusion immediately after the crash it was not too difficult for him to hide it, temporarily, in the soft sand.

After the area had been cleared of wreckage and when it was safe to do so, the tank was quietly recovered and taken to a farm some miles away. The farm belonged to a friend of the policeman and there the two men began the job of transferring the fuel, amounting to almost 45 gallons, into a multitude of containers — cans, drums, jars etc. These containers were then carefully hidden in the farm outbuildings, eventually to be shared between the two friends.

P.C. 'X' owned an Austin 7 motor car and was keen to make use of his newly found fuel source at the first opportunity. He decided to take his wife on a trip to Llandudno and so he filled the tank of his car with fuel from the crashed Beaufighter despite his friend's advice that high octane aviation fuel was not very suitable for the car's engine and might even damage it. Mixing oil with the fuel might help to prevent damage it was suggested but the advice went unheeded.

On the journey to Llandudno the little Austin's performance proved to be spectacular, much to the satisfaction of its driver. Apparently, the car went "like a bloody rocket!"

However, the return journey proved to be very different. Firstly, the engine would not start and it was only after much expenditure of energy and cursing that it was eventually persuaded to fire. Having succeeded in starting the engine P.C. 'X' thought his troubles were over, but it was not to be. After leaving Llandudno he quickly became aware that the car was lacking in power and furthermore its condition seemed to be worsening by the mile.

As the villages of Penmaenmawr and Llanfairfechan went by, the little Austin became ever more sluggish. To make matters worse P.C 'X' noticed the exhaust of his car was emitting quantities of blue smoke. There was no doubt about it, something was wrong. Soon a lower gear had to be selected and by the time Anglesey was reached the car was incapable of anything better than a 15 m.p.h. crawl in low gear.

Upon inspection the engine was found to have suffered major damage with burnt out valves and badly scored cylinder walls. Such was the price P.C. 'X' had to pay for his misdeeds!

But to return to the story of 456 Squadron, on 8th December 1941 two raiders came into the sector. Squadron Leader Dottridge was given vectors for one raider, which he intercepted, but the aircraft dived from 13,000 feet to 3,000 feet and escaped. Another was intercepted by Flying Officer Pargeter and pursued as far as the Humber without being caught.

The squadron's disappointment increased next day when, in poor weather, raiders attacked a convoy in the Irish Sea, having flown in low, thereby avoiding radar and visual detection. As the cloud base was down to 200 feet and visibility one mile, 456's aircraft had to remain grounded, giving rise to a maddening feeling of helplessness amongst the crews.

A day fighter squadron was also formed at Valley in 1941 — No.350 (Belgian) Squadron under the command of Squadron Leader J. M. Thompson. The new squadron flew Spitfire Mk.IIs paid for by donations to the Belgian Congo Fighter Fund, with each aircraft bearing the name of a prominent Belgian district, town or personality. Belgian pilots were drawn from two flights of 131 Squadron, other areas of Fighter Command and those who escaped to Britain from their homeland to form the new squadron.

Aircrew began arriving in mid November and as most were experienced the squadron was not long in becoming operational. Its duties were routine convoy patrols. On 12th February 1942 an inaugeration ceremony took place at Northolt in the presence of Sir Archibald Sinclair, Secretary of State for Air, Msr. Gutt, Minister of National Defence in the Belgian Government, Prince Bernhardt of the Netherlands, Sir Sholto Douglas and many other top ranking officers of the Allied air forces. The squadron was inspected by Sir Archibald Sinclair and the ceremony ended with a fly past. In the evening dinner was given at the Savoy Hotel to Belgian pilots serving in the RAF.

On the following day 350 Squadron returned to Valley and was soon back on routine Irish Sea patrols. Within three days however the squadron was posted to Atcham.

Other units based for short periods at Valley during 1941 were two sections of Hurricanes from 302 Squadron and one flight of Spitfires from 403 Squadron, in June and July respectively, and Hurricanes from 605 Squadron and 43 Squadron in September.

Meanwhile, Valley's night fighter squadron, No. 456, had its first victory on 10th January 1942 when Squadron Leader J. Hamilton and Pilot officer D. Norris-Smith were scrambled at 10.00 p.m. to intercept six enemy aircraft suspected of laying mines in the sea approaches to Liverpool. Hamilton kept losing contact with the raiders due to poor communications with GCI Trewan Sands, arising from faulty R/T equipment, but eventually GCI Hack Green took over the interception control, improving communications considerably. A few minutes before midnight Hamilton made contact with a Dornier DO217 at 12,000 feet and after a seven minute chase shot it down with two bursts of cannon fire.

After this success a long period of inactivity followed, with nothing but training and routine patrols taking place. This, not surprisingly, had an adverse affect on morale, with the squadron being described by disgruntled pilots as "nothing more than just a glorified OTU".

The situation improved a little in May, when on the 18th Pilot Officer Wills and Sergeant Lowther, whilst on convoy patrol in St. George's Channel identified a JU88 flying in cloud. They gave chase for 20 minutes, playing hide and seek in the clouds before the Beaufighter succeeded in closing to firing range. Wills gave the JU88 three bursts of cannon fire which his observer saw striking the aircraft just before it disappeared once again into cloud. No further contact was made and so the claim by Pilot Officer Wills was 'damaged' only, but a few days later No.9 Group Intelligence received information that the JU88 had been destroyed after crashing in the sea twenty five miles west of Bardsey.

This interception took place in daylight as the squadron had been on day readiness for some time. Not everyone agreed with this policy, some pilots arguing that because of the difficulty of making interceptions by day with the comparatively slow Beaufighter, no useful purpose could be served by day readiness. Pilot Officer Wills' success seemed to prove otherwise.

On the 20th 456 was again operational against hostile raids by day but no visual contacts were made, which might have given a little satisfaction to the critics of daylight operations.

The squadron had a bad day on 26th June when an aircraft was lost to enemy fire. Pilot Officer Day and Sergeant Mitchell were scrambled at 11.45 a.m. to intercept a lone JU88 30 miles west of Bardsey but in the ensuing fight accurate fire from the JU88 stopped the Beaufighter's port engine and severed a fuel line, causing the cockpit to fill with petrol. Day was forced to ditch his aircraft, which sank within minutes. Sergeant Mitchell's dinghy failed to inflate and so he had no alternative but to share Pilot Officer Day's dinghy. Both men were suffering from the effects of immersion and exposure by the time they were rescued ninety minutes later. As the squadron diary recorded, "One for the Germans!"

A chance to even the score arose on 27th July when eight enemy bombers appeared over Cardigan Bay but unfortunately thirty OTU bombers were also in the area on exercise, causing great confusion on radar plots. Wing Commander Wolfe, 456's CO, obtained three contacts, two of which turned out to be friendly and one doubtful. Other pilots, to their great disappointment, had no contacts at all.

Three nights later Wing Commander Wolfe and Pilot Officer Ashcroft took off from Valley shortly after midnight to patrol Cardigan Bay. Whilst over the Llŷn peninsula they were given vectors for two enemy aircraft but as OTU bombers were still on exercise Wolfe was extremely cautious. Having made contact with the nearest of the two aircraft he carefully identified it as a JU88 before launching an attack. However, the German pilot had seen the Beaufighter and through violent manoeuvering managed to shake off his pursuer.

Wolfe now turned his attention to the second raider, still in the vicinity. After obtaining a visual sighting at 2,000 feet range he identified it as a Heinkel HEIII. Closing to 250 yards he fired two short bursts causing the Heinkel to hastily jettison its bomb load. More gunfire resulted in flames appearing from the bomber. Wolfe then broke off his attack and watched the stricken aircraft go into an increasingly steep dive from 2,000 feet to crash and explode on Pwllheli beach. Two men had baled out and were later picked up from the sea but the other crew members died in the crash. This Heinkel (coded F8+LW) was, in fact, the last German aircraft shot down in North Wales.

Another squadron which spent a short period of time at Valley during 1942 was 131 Squadron, which moved from Llanbedr early in March in order to operate patrols in the Irish Sea. As soon as it arrived the squadron began to suffer from the effects of wind-blown sand which found its way into the guns and engines of the squadron's Spitfires with remorseless efficiency. This caused endless and extremely frustrating serviceability problems. Indeed, poor serviceability bedevilled all squadrons operating from Valley until the sand problem was solved.

The squadron was operational on 12th March when Flight Lieutenant R. Harries and Sergeant Vilboux (Free French Air Force) were ordered to scramble and intercept a JU88 thirty five miles south west of Valley. They successfully attacked the raider, at the price of a few bullet holes in Fl.Lt. Harries' Spitfire. The JU88 with both engines on fire crashed into the sea with no survivors.

During April the squadron took part in an unusual Army co-operation exercise at an encampment near Portmadoc — a beat up of Army horses and mules in order to assess the effect of diving aircraft on their behaviour. Contrary to expectations, the results revealed no adverse effects on the animals. They all remained calm!

But by mid April sand had defeated 131 Squadron. The problem had become so acute, with aircraft engines having to be overhauled far more frequently than was normally the case, that hasty arrangements were made to return to Llanbedr immediately.

On 1st May Valley had a new CO, Wing Commander W. Churchill, DSO, DFC, and sand soon loomed large in his life also. He wrote, one week after taking up his post, ". . .had a busy first week at Valley making detailed inspections of the camp and formulating schemes to combat the biggest enemy — SAND — . . ."

After discussions on how to deal with this serious problem, one suggestion was to dredge silt from nearby lakes and spread it over the airfield. This simple remedy was put into effect and to the relief of all concerned it was found to work very well, stabilising the sand most effectively. It allowed grass to grow which in turn caused further stabilisation of the soil. One totally unexpected result of the dredging operation was to reveal a major archaeological find in the lake known as Llyn Cerrig Bach.

This exciting and spectacular discovery consisted of an accumulation of objects described by an expert as: "one of the most important collections of Iron Age material in Western Europe". Another result of putting silt on the airfield was to stimulate the growth of particularly large and tasty mushrooms!

No.315 (Polish) Squadron was another short stay resident at Valley, from May until September 1942. On 23rd August the squadron's Spitfires engaged a JU88 near Dublin, killing the rear gunner and inflicting damage which caused the aircraft to make a forced landing near Wexford. This combat ended in a draw as one of the Spitfires was also shot down; its Polish pilot, Flying Officer Sawiak, later died from his injuries. In September another detachment of Hurricanes from 247 Squadron, High Ercall, took over from 315 Squadron until February 1943.

Other developments during September and October 1942 included approval for a 360 yard extension to the southern end of the NW-SE runway, bringing it to a total length of 1,960 yards and extension of the N-S runway from 1,300 yards to 1,400 yards in a northerly direction. In addition, ground at both ends of the NE-SW runway was levelled to make overshooting and undershooting less hazardous.

Also in September a small air-to-ground firing range was being prepared at Carmel Head on the north east coast of Anglesey, for use by visiting squadrons in conjunction with 1486 Fighter Gunnery Flight. This unit had two Martinets, two Masters and three Lysanders when it arrived at Valley in February 1942.

Another non-operational but very important unit formed at Valley on 15th October 1941 was No.275 ASR Squadron, (ASR – Air Sea Rescue). The war had resulted in enormous growth of the RAF organisation for rescuing ditched aircrew which did much to improve morale.

Valley's ASR squadron, as part of this growing organisation, was responsible for many rescues in the Irish Sea and Cardigan Bay. The squadron was equipped at first with Lysanders and Walruses but later Ansons, Defiants, and Spitfires were flown, the latter type in the search role whilst Ansons were used for supply and dinghy dropping.

Undoubtedly there was a real need for such a squadron because of the large number of crashes and ditchings that took place. In June 1942 for example, besides the usual training and exercise flights, 275 Squadron was actively searching for ditched aircraft on ten occasions:

1st June — search for Fulmar aircraft in Liverpool Bay
6th June — search for Wellington aircraft
8th June — search for Anson aircraft off Tŷ Croes
11th June — search for Anson aircraft off Llandwrog (Walrus landed)
11th June — search for Manchester aircraft off Rhyl
15th June — search for a dinghy
19th June — search for Wellington aircraft
22nd June — search for Anson aircraft
23rd June — search for Anson aircraft
29th June — search for Walrus landed south of Isle of Man to pick up Spitfire pilot.

The squadron suffered its own casualties some-times too, as on 7th May 1943, when Pilot Officer Furlong whilst practising sea landings in his Walrus two miles off the north of Anglesey got into difficulties because of heavy seas and cross winds. The aircraft lost a float, capsized, and then sank. An Anson was also lost in July after crashing in the sea, but luckily with no casualties. The squadron eventually moved to Warmwell, Dorset, in April 1944.

Meanwhile, Valley's longest serving fighter squadron, 456, after Wing Commander Wolfe's success in July 1942 was having a lean time with no enemy activity at all in the sector. The squadron had to content itself with routine patrols, exercises, long distance training flights, calibration runs for GCI stations and developing new techniques of co-operation with searchlight units. During the summer of 1942 the squadron was re-equipped with the Beaufighter Mk.VI, powered by Hercules radial engines. In August, after being operational for only a few weeks, these aircraft were re-camouflaged. Previously they were matt black all over but this, as it turned out, made them easier to see at night, in contrast to aircraft with normal day camouflage. Upper surfaces were therefore repainted dark green/ocean grey whilst undersurfaces remained matt black.

However, the squadron was not to have these aircraft for very long. In December 1942 news was received that Mosquitos were to replace them, the first being delivered to Valley before the month was out. Conversion to type was carried out in January, smoothly and efficiently, in contrast to the difficulties experienced converting from Defiants to Beaufighters fifteen months previously. At the end of March 456 Squadron transferred to Middle Wallop. Prior to moving, the squadron commander gave Valley faint praise when he wrote, "it hasn't been a bad place, but we have been here such a long time (21 months) that the change will do everyone good".

Before leaving 456 it is perhaps worth quoting two items from the squadron diary which reveal a touch of humour in what can sometimes be a dry, official record. The entry for 19th May 1942, for instance, reads, "Gas practice carried out and some illegitimate place a tear gas generator outside the window of the Officers Mess during breakfast and everybody cried into their porridge!"

Then this description of an accident on 20th March 1942 — "15.15 hours, Sergeant Spring in T3012 swung to port (third solo in Beaufighter). The port wing struck the post supporting the windsock, resulting in the wing being torn off. The aircraft rolled for 300 yards and burst into flames. . .It provided a spectacular firework display, a Brocks Benefit as cannon shells and tanks burst. The fire engine was unable to do anything because of flying shrapnel, and so covered itself with foam instead (due to an airman manipulating the hose and inadvertently turning it towards the engine!)" The pilot suffered burns but they were not serious.

Next at Valley was 406 (RCAF) Squadron, equipped with the Mark VI Beaufighter. The squadron was commanded by Wing Commander I. R. Stephenson. There was no hint of enemy activity however, and so, besides routine patrols 406's pilots had little to do but take part in exercises, for example, making practice low level attacks on troops and army vehicles near Newborough and Aberffraw.

Another task, in May, was to impart the squadron's expertise and operational techniques to an USAAF unit, the 414th Night Fighter Squadron, from Honiley. This unit flew Beaufighter MK.VIFs and remained at Valley for eleven days.

But these diversions did not make up for the lack of real operational flying, and so, like other units previously at Valley, morale suffered as a result. After seven months of patrols, tests, training and exercise, news of a transfer to Exeter in November 1943 was greeted with joy. The CO wrote, "We will hope to have more opportunity to live up to the squadron motto — 'We Kill by Night' ". Certainly Valley had not offered this chance.

In fact by late 1943 enemy activity in the sector was over for good and there would be no action for 406's successor either. This was No.125 Squadron, which arrived from Exeter in mid-November. Early in 1944 the squadron re-equipped with Mosquitos prior to departing for Hurn in March. This departure, to all intents and purposes brought to an end Valley's role as a fighter station.

When compared with other airfields it must be said that Valley never was a focus of action in the same way that the more well known airfields of south east England, for instance, had been. Enemy activity in the north west sector, of which Valley was the operational centre, was too sporadic for that, and as a result many of the fighter squadrons operating here found themselves with too many routine patrols and exercises for their liking.

Low morale was a consequence of this inactivity, which is understandable, as most fighter pilots, being combative by nature, would prefer to get to grips with the enemy rather than champ at the bit in a quiet sector.

Nevertheless, as a result of their time in Gwynedd a number of squadrons could claim definite 'kills'. For instance, 219 Squadron shot down one JU88 as did 131 Squadron; 68 Squadron claimed one Heinkel HE111 and 456 Squadron claimed a Dornier DO 217, a JU88 and a Heinkel HE111. In addition, many other interceptions by these squadrons, and others, resulted in damage to enemy aircraft.

With this period of Valley's history over by the end of 1943 the stage had already been set for another major and important development — the airfield's use as a transatlantic terminal for American aircraft.

Chapter 3

Transatlantic Terminal
R.A.F. Valley 1943-1945

The summer of 1943 can be regarded as a turning point in the wartime history of Valley. From then onwards its role as an operational fighter station steadily diminished in importance as enemy activity in the sector dwindled to nothing, and as the chances of any further raids or attacks became increasingly remote so it became less necessary to provide fighter cover for the region.

Whilst some might have regretted this decline in activity, to the Air Ministry and those within the Air Transport Command of the USAAF it was fortunate and most convenient because it facilitated the station's change of role to that of a terminal for US bombers crossing the Atlantic to join operational squadrons in England.

This scheme, known as Operation Transat, was by far the largest single wartime development at any of Gwynedd's airfields and resulted in much upheaval and organisational change. From July 1943 RAF units at Valley took second place as the American presence came to dominate.

Once the scheme was in operation heavy bombers of the US Eighth Air Force, mostly B-24 Liberators and B-17 Fortresses, began to flow into the airfield in ever increasing numbers. They would have a brief stay before taking off again for their final destinations, usually bomber airfields in East Anglia. This influx continued as the bombing offensive against Germany built up, and was maintained until the war ended. Then in May 1945 the flow of aircraft into Valley was reversed as bombers used the airfield as a point of departure for their homeward journey back to the United States.

Ensuring the efficient and smooth running of Operation Transat presented many organisational problems and challenges to the Americans and their RAF colleagues, which in the main were fully met, as the following pages will reveal.

One of the first indications of Valley's future use as a transatlantic base was a somewhat prophetic memo sent from the Senior Aerodrome Control Officer to the Station Commander in December 1941 outlining some of the problems associated with an anticipated increase in diversions of American aircraft from Prestwick in 1942.

RAF records reveal that on 30th March 1942 Valley received a communication from the Air Ministry, via 44 Group that American heavy bombers totalling 128 aircraft had been or would be, departing the US for Britain. Although it was not clear if Valley was to be used as a diversionary base it was assumed that this was the case at the airfield itself and preparations were put in hand to receive the aircraft and their crews.

Next, Headquarters No.9 Group informed Valley in April that, "From the 15th May 1942 and at intervals thereafter, an American Air Corps Bomber Group not exceeding in number thirty-two Boeing B-17 or Consolidated B-24 aircraft with a crew of nine personnel per aircraft and some passengers, may at short notice be diverted to RAF Station Valley".

At once, since domestic accommodation was already short, arrangements were put in hand to obtain the necessary stores and equipment for a tent encampment for the crews and to give first priority to the construction of hardstandings for aircraft.

It is not clear how much traffic was actually diverted from Prestwick, but it must be concluded that some aircraft were sent because of hints in RAF records of constant anxiety over the prospect and problems of expansion.

Responsibility for transport and ferrying lay with Transport Command's No.44 Group and in June 1942 a memo from Group HQ to HQ Fighter Command (who controlled Valley) stated, "That the Air Ministry propose according a high priority to the construction of the necessary hardstandings and appropriate action will be taken immediately".

By the end of July another stage in the development had been completed according to a letter from the Air Ministry to HQ 44 Group which reveals that "agreement is given in principle to Valley Station being No.1 Primary Diversional Alternative. The effective use of Valley would appear to depend on the construction of hardstanding aprons . . ."

"The provision of these hardstandings, dispersal points and existing aprons has been agreed in principle and the Works Directorate are proceeding with the preparations of final details, with a view to the work being put in hand".

Now, as mentioned previously, Valley was under the control of No.9 Group, Fighter Command, and those wishing to see the airfield used as an alternative to Prestwick, i.e. the Americans, Transport Command and the Air Ministry had first to gain the co-operation and agreement of Fighter Command to these changes.

On 28th September 1942 the proposals for 'Operation Transat' were put formally by the Air Ministry to Fighter Command. The document stated that a second transatlantic terminal was needed to supplement Prestwick and as a bad weather alternative. Hitherto Squires Gate at

Blackpool performed this function but it was becoming increasingly unsatisfactory (for reasons not given). Another airfield had to be found which met six requirements:-

    1) located on the west coast
    2) have good road and rail communications
    3) possess a good weather record
    4) located near to the US depots at Warton and Burtonwood
    5) possess good runways, capable of extension if necessary
    6) in an area free of obstructions

Valley met all six requirements the Ministry said and therefore it was ideal for use as a transatlantic terminal. Special facilities were needed, such as customs, security, extra navigational aids, telecommunications etc. Up to a maximum of forty aircraft per day could be expected and accommodation for fifty permanent staff and up to two hundred aircrew, in transit, had to be found. Runway extensions for which HQ Fighter Command was already seeking Air Ministry approval would become a matter of priority.

Early in October Fighter Command's C. in C., Air Chief Marshall Sholto Douglas agreed to the proposals and replied to the Air Ministry, "I have considered your request and I agree to Valley being used as a second Trans-Atlantic Air Base. The full accommodation for aircraft and personnel should now be worked out between Air Ministry and Fighter Command."

"It will be necessary to retain the existing permanent accommodation at Valley for:-

    1) 1 twin engined night fighter squadron
    2) the Air/Sea Rescue squadron (275 Squadron)
    3) small detachment of approx. three aircraft and twenty five airmen of the T.F.U. (the Telecommunications Flying Unit at RAF Defford, Worcs. who used Valley as a base for experimental flights over the sea, testing equipment for Coastal Command).

"I will move the No.9 Group Gunnery Flight (1486 Flight) now at Valley, to Llanbedr".

From then on a number of meetings and conferences took place to solve the organisational problems. For instance, a meeting in November 1942 noted that runways could be extended up to 3,000 yards and that the N-S strip, the extension of which to 1,400 yards had been sanctioned, could be further extended to 1,600 yards fairly easily and 1,786 yards if problems created by construction on marshland at the northern end could be overcome.

The main difficulty facing RAF and USAAF planners seemed to be that of providing accommodation for the expected influx of transient American aircrews without recourse to an expensive building programme.

During the same month the local HQ of the Air Ministry Works Directorate, at Llanwnda near Caernarfon, produced a £60,000 estimate for the proposed extension to the perimeter track and construction of hardstandings etc. The expenditure was approved and the work carried out, eventually.

Meanwhile, on the other side of the Atlantic a meeting took place in November 1942 at Dorval Aerodrome, Montreal, between officers from the RAF's Transport Command and the US Air Transport Command to discuss the development of an American A.T.C. wing on British soil. It was decided that Prestwick would retain its dominant role and in addition to Valley, RAF stations at St. Mawgan, Cornwall and Nutts Corner in Northern Ireland would also be utilised by the Americans as air bases.

A second meeting was held in Washington D.C. in December which laid down policy and a Joint Board of American and British Officers was set up to implement the policy. In February 1943 a headquarters was established in London and designated European Division, Air Transport Command.

One of its first acts was to organise an inspection tour of the UK and a party visited Valley in March 1943 to consider technical problems, e.g. signals, weather forecasting facilities, radio communications etc.

But how to provide domestic accommodation without incurring expense remained the biggest problem. It was decided that by some squeezing and crowding a number in excess of 600 Americans could be accommodated in existing quarters since RAF strength was less than the maximum allowable figure.

However, by March senior officers at Fighter Command had become rather worried at the way development was progressing and some disagreement arose as a result.

For instance, a divergence of views occurred over the necessity or otherwise of transferring Valley from Fighter Command to Transport Command. Air Commodore Kingston-McLoughry, AOC 44 Group, Transport Command, had requested the transfer on the grounds that his organisation would bear the major responsibility and that Fighter Command should become a lodger unit on the airfield. Furthermore, because of this commitment, said the Air Commodore, Valley's CO should be of Group Captain rank.

This request was passed via the Air Ministry, which agreed with the proposal, and was then presented to Fighter Command early in March 1943. Not surprisingly it met with little enthusiasm. The Command's senior officers took themselves to be under threat of eviction from an operational station which they were loath to give up. On 9th March the Deputy Senior Air Staff Officer, clearly in a state of anger, wrote to his immediate superior setting out objections and also revealing a little of the rivalry that existed between Commands:-

SASO
1. . . .I am strongly opposed to the suggestion. . .by which we shall lose operational control of the aerodrome at Valley.
2. When Air Ministry first asked us to let them have Valley as a standby Transatlantic base to be used only for peak periods and when weather conditions were unsuitable at Prestwick, they assured us that we should retain operational control of this aerodrome. . .They added a little soft soap. . .in view of the importance of getting American aircraft across the Atlantic we agreed to Valley being used by No.44 Group. . .
3. This was evidently only the thin end of the wedge and 44 Group having laid their talons on Valley, now propose to seize it for their own use and gradually oust us out of it.
4. We require Valley for the following purposes:-
   a) Accommodation for a Night Fighter squadron
   b) Accommodation for a proportion of No.275 Air Sea Rescue Squadron
   c) No.9 Group Gunnery Flight
5. . . .the late C.in C. agreed to move No.9 Group Gunnery Flight, now at Valley, to Llanbedr, but it is the present C.in C.'s intention to retain the existing Flight at Valley for use by No.9 Group squadrons and Night Fighter Squadrons in other Groups, Llanbedr being used to accommodate the Gunnery Flight now in Northern Ireland and to be used by 14 Day Squadrons in No.11 Group. We shall, therefore, require Valley accommodation for an additional Night Fighter Squadron when these Squadrons go there in rotation to complete their gunnery training.
6. I realise that the Sector at Valley is being given up and absorbed into

the Woodvale Sector and that therefore the Station Commander need only be a Wing Commander. I suggest, however, that rather than give this Station up to 44 Group we should upgrade it to be commanded by a Group Captain as he will have quite a responsible job to look after all the Fighter Command Units stationed there, i.e. 2 night fighter squadrons, a Gunnery Flight and a detachment of the Air Sea Rescue Squadron plus the men required to handle the Transatlantic traffic. You will note that. . .again Air Ministry state that 44 Group will only require the existing Flying Control staff to be supplemented by the Liason Officer and the appropriate Flying Control officers from 44 Group.

7. . . .
8. . . .
9. . . .
10. Other points which require consideration are that Valley is an important aerodrome for the defence of Liverpool and to some extent Northern Ireland, and in addition it enjoys very good weather and is useful to get aircraft down on when other parts of the country are out of action. These are additional reasons for retaining it as a Fighter Command Station."

When speaking of the 'thin end of the wedge' the deputy SASO was in fact correct — for Fighter Command it was indeed the beginning of the end at Valley. But that end came about not through some kind of conspiracy, as suggested, but rather because of the process of adaption to changing circumstances of war.

On 15th March Air Marshall Leigh Mallory, C. in C. Fighter Command, after some consideration, refused to approve the transfer of Valley to Transport Command but agreed that construction work to meet the 'Transat' scheme requirements could continue provided that Fighter Command facilities were fully embodied in the plan, i.e. one night fighter squadron (456 Sqdn.), 275 ASR Sqdn., 1486 Gunnery Flight, a twin engined squadron on a reduced basis carrying out gunnery training (414th USAAF) and lastly the TFU detachment.

The Air Ministry agreed to retention of Fighter Command control over Valley and its operational units there with the exception of the gunnery flights and TFU detachment which should be moved elsewhere it was suggested. For the time being it seemed that 44 Group had failed to gain control of the airfield!

Whilst these high level discussions were taking place many site conferences were also being held to reach agreement on matters of detail and by the time the last of these was held, in June 1943, great changes were evident. Practically the whole of the station was re-organised in one way or another. Runways had been extended, hardstandings constructed, bulk fuel installations capacity increased from 108,000 gallons to 180,000 gallons to meet increased demand, navigational aids were installed and Fighter Command had vacated some parts of the airfield leaving three large dispersal areas for development by Transport Command and the USAAF although the problem of accommodation had still not been adequately solved.

Two units were posted in accordance with Air Ministry wishes, 414th USAAF went to Honiley in May and 1486 Gunnery Flight to Llanbedr in July.

On 17th June the Americans finally arrived. To quote USAAF records, "Major Jerry B. Sass, the first American C.O. at Valley and Lts. Clifford and Kurtz arrived (from the USAAF unit at Stone, Staffs) at the base, with 86 men, trailing behind them an endless line of vehicles of various sorts to the amazement of the surprised RAF and WAAF personnel already on the field. The officers were billeted initially with RAF officers whilst the enlisted men were given somewhat inadequate accommodation on Site 7 (on the north west side of the airfield), the buildings of which were in bad repair, unheated and without water or latrines".

One sergeant recorded his first impressions as follows — "Our first sight of Valley was slightly depressing. To begin with, we were six hours by the fastest train from London, the centre of all our pleasures. Secondly, we were met at the station by an over-hospitable cold front which gave us a very damp hello. When the rain let up sufficiently to make possible a quick look around, we discovered that our range of vision was approximately forty miles in every direction. Trees and hills had apparently departed with the Druids and had left only miles and more miles of flat, bare country.

"We were, however, somewhat consoled when we learned of a lovely, sandy bathing beach on the camp proper, [i.e. Cymyran Beach], populated throughout the summer by an abundance of sun-tanned bathing beauties, reputedly fit subjects for a Varga or Petty drawing, and with these mingled opinions of our new station we retired to the comforts of our Nissen Hut for the night."

As mentioned previously, proper accommodation remained an unsolved problem and at first, but temporarily only, American officers shared the RAF Officers Mess. It was felt, certainly by the British, that a separate Mess would be better given the differing traditions between the two groups and eventually a new Mess was constructed for the Americans.

But the enlisted men on the other hand had to be content with field conditions, more or less. Although a building programme was under way the rate of progress was much too slow for the Americans and with typical 'get up and go' spirit they set about building their own Mess Hall and Billets on Site No.7, laying down water pipes, providing latrines etc., improvising where necessary and obtaining materials from a variety of (undisclosed) sources! Three weeks after starting work the men were eating American food in their own Mess Hall and in addition, "The water line had been accomplished by almost two weeks of continual blasting thru solid rock, sewerage disposal system had been set up and supplies were coming in quickly, with good co-operation from the RAF".

Meanwhile, other sections were arriving, e.g. on 23rd June detachment 'F' of the 24th Region, Army Airways Communication System and on the same day the Motor Pool. Two officers and eight men arrived to set up the Weather Station on 1st July and a PX was operating by the 2nd. Throughout July arrivals increased the unit strength to 19 officers and 163 men.

It must be said though that some of the GIs who found themselves at Valley were not amongst the cream of the Air Force. A few had been rejected by other units and had nowhere else to go. A Lt. Keenan, for example, arrived from Prestwick to take charge of the Engineering Section accompanied by, "65 cast-off, prejudiced, untried, but willing enlisted mechanics". At first their equipment consisted of, "4 or 5 bicycles and 2 Crewchief Kits"!

Coinciding with Lt. Keenan's arrival urgent requests were made to the RAF for hangar facilities. In addition the steady arrival of men necessitated more billet accommodation. Thus Fighter and Transport Commands, and the Air Ministry held a meeting on 12th July at which the following decisions were reached:

1) to give up two Bellman hangars to the USAAF as soon as possible, and as many Blisters as necessary
2) to provide the USAAF as much comfort as possible within the limitations of works services on sites 6 and 7
3) ultimately to vacate WAAF sites 4, 4B and 4C, which would be handed over to the Americans

Thus, with inadequate accommodation, lack of equipment and properly trained men, improvisation was very much the order of the day, and to return to Lt. Keenan's mechanics, "They proved willing members, anxious to dispel the cloud which Prestwick had held over

45

them, therefore, before there were any American aircraft on the field, they — together with other enlisted men — might have been seen working earnestly throughout the base, building benches, desks, and racks from emptied packing cases, stringing electrical connections, installing stoves, sweeping, cleaning, preparing in countless ways for the routine work which lay ahead".

On 17th July, as expected, the Station Commander, Wing Commander H.N.G. Ramsbottom-Isherwood, DFC, AFC, received his promotion to Group Captain. His primary consideration now was to balance the needs of both RAF and USAAF units, ensuring a harmonious relationship between the two. A Fighter Command memo stated, "The CO is going to have a difficult time as Valley will be a huge transatlantic terminal aerodrome. . .receiving a continual stream of passengers will tax the organising ability of the CO to the utmost." It is fair to say that Group Captain Ramsbottom-Isherwood succeeded admirably.

Also in July Major Sass departed, to be replaced by Lt. Col. James C. Cochran and in August the unit was re-designated from Army Air Force Station 1005 to the 1407th AAF Air Base Unit, European Division, Air Transport Command.

The first two months were operationally quiet, most of the time being spent on setting up the organisation.

The men of the Weather Section in particular seemed to have found their surroundings most congenial. They shared facilities with RAF staff which, to quote the Americans, "was composed of eight lovely young WAAFS who spurred us on to eager plotting by their charm — also their cooking. Frequently, throughout the long vigil of a graveyard shift we would be revived from the coma caused by pressures and isobars with a steaming cup of coffee — granted it was a bit chicorish — and now and then, as a surprise, fresh eggs on toast. After such treatment we returned to our labours with a gusto rarely seen in any weather station". Inevitably in such circumstances romance blossomed and in September 1944 one of the GIs married a WAAF.

The first American aircraft to land at Valley under the 'Transat' operation was B-17 No.42-30504 piloted by Lt. Kidman, which arrived direct from Newfoundland on the morning of 25th July 1943 after an uneventful crossing of the Atlantic. In August eleven Liberators of the US Navy arrived from Iceland en route to St. Eval in Cornwall.

From that time onwards the base began to receive aircraft in increasing numbers. The month of September, for example, saw the following arrivals:-

6th — 2 B-24s from Iceland
11th — 5 B-24s from Iceland
12th — 2 B-25s and 3 C-47s from Stornoway
14th — 1 B-24 from Marrakech
15th — 1 B-25, 5 PB47s and 6 B-24s from Iceland
17th — 2 B-24s from Iceland, 6 C-47s and 1 C-53 from Stornoway
18th — 10 C-47s from Stornoway
19th — 5 PB47s and 5 B-24s from Iceland
21st — 1 C-47, 1 B-25 and 1 B-26 from Stornoway
25th — 1 PB47 from Iceland

These aircraft and the hundreds that followed over the coming months arrived by flying one of two routes across the Atlantic — a northern and a southern route, the latter being used mostly to avoid the harsher northern weather especially during winter. Aircraft flying the northern route usually began their journey from Dow Field and Presque Isle in Maine. Facilities were then available at Goose Bay in Labrador, Bluie West 1 in Greenland, Meeks Field in Iceland, Stephenville and Gander, both in Newfoundland. Lagens, a base in the Azores was also available.

Starting point for those taking the southern route was Morrison Field, Miami, then Borinquen (Puerto Rico), Waller Field (Trinidad), Atkinson Field (British Guiana), Belem and Natal (Brazil), Dakar (French West Africa) and Marrakech in French Morocco.

These flights presented many hazards, e.g. long periods over water: 1,200 miles from Natal to Dakar for instance; lack of navigational aids and variable weather, whilst on the last stages of the southern route from Dakar onwards there was the danger of false radio signals sent out by the Germans to lure aircraft inland, in addition to the risk of attack by patrolling Junkers JU88s especially in the Bay of Biscay area. This happened on 18th November 1943 when B-24 42-7512 was attacked by two JU88s and a Focke Wulf 189. Luckily the Liberator was able to drive off its attackers though one of its engines had been stopped. The aircraft was eventually met and escorted into Valley by a Beaufighter of the resident 406 Squadron.

At any one time there would be large numbers of aircraft parked, as the record for 17th October shows. . . "there were 57 US heavies on the Western perimeter track today, and hardstandings near the technical site. All difficulties of feeding, fuelling, accommodation etc. successfully overcome."

One American commented, "As the Fall came on, planes began to arrive more frequently, at first in little groups, but gradually growing into rather impressive armadas. It became a familiar and heartening sight to see lines of gray Fortresses lined up along our perimeter tracks."

Also, late October marked the start of internal shuttle operations whereby Dakotas would fly between London (Hendon) and other American unit locations at Valley, Nutts Corner and Prestwick. This shuttle was soon nicknamed 'The Marble Arch Airline'.

Whilst the 'Transat' scheme expanded, on the RAF side Valley's role as an active fighter station diminished. From 1st November 1943 the airfield ceased to be a sector station and all personnel involved were transferred to Woodvale which took over control of the sector. Trewan Sand GCI station remained open however. In November the 'Q' site at Newborough Warren was abandoned as no longer serving any useful purpose.

The total number of American aircraft handled in 1943 was 365 - 226 four engined 'heavies' and 139 twin engined aircraft. The crews of four engined aircraft were usually operational, or replacement crews who would leave their aircraft and proceed to the Eighth Air Force Replacement Centre at Stone, Staffs. On the other hand twin engined aircraft were flown by ferrying crews, who once they had delivered one aircraft would return to the United States to pick up another. They went via Prestwick, either travelling to Scotland by train or whenever possible by air using the 'Marble Arch' shuttle.

Most of the aircraft left at Valley were then picked up by crews of the Eighth and Ninth Air Force Transport Group for ferrying to the major US bases at Warton or Burtonwood in Lancashire before delivery to an operational unit. Soon after the system was operating an innovative development was to introduce a Lead aircraft from an UK base to 'shepherd' other aircraft to their destinations. Volume of traffic and American crews' unfamiliarity with British procedures and weather was the reason for this system, which generally worked well.

With the turn of the year operational activity became steadily more and more intense with traffic flow increasing continually until July 1944. The figures in summary are:-

	4 engined aircraft	twin engined aircraft
January 1944	143	43
February	149	204 (of which 62 C47s landed from Marrakech in one day)
March	322	132

(In April news was received that "War Weary" Flying Fortresses were to be returned to the U.S. for modification or disposal, through Valley and then via the southern route)

	4 engined aircraft	twin engined aircraft
April	389 53 War Wearies	165
May	458 26 War Wearies	110
June	302 16 War Wearies	107
July	530 16 War Wearies	109 16 single engined aircraft

Meanwhile, building of accommodation for transit crews was being hurried as much as possible but was still not completed by early 1944, forcing the Americans to improvise when large numbers of aircraft arrived. On 17th February for instance 62 C-47s turned up, their crews being accommodated in the gymnasium and concert hall, and as the station diary records, "by filling up every available corner".

The safety record for American aircraft had been extremely good with no crashes on the airfield but one did occur in bad weather to a B-24 in the hills of Snowdonia on 7th January 1944. This crash is described in detail in Chapter 9. Another example of bad weather causing problems occurred on 29th March 1944 when a C-47 was unable to locate Valley in low cloud and rain, and as a result crashed near the Great Orme but luckily without injury to the crew. It was one of 73 flying from Marrakech. Of the rest one B-24 and 24 C-47s found the airfield — 3 others landed at Mona and the remainder at St. Mawgan, Turnberry and West Freugh. One B-24 crashed at Fairwood Common.

By June construction of Nissen Huts eased the acute accommodation problem for transit crews and completion of large concrete hardstandings on the airfield's western side provided extra space for parking scores of heavy bombers arriving at frequent intervals. Ample space existed for a hundred of these aircraft at Valley plus their crews.

But accommodation for some of the permanent American sections remained unsatisfactory, mainly because of their dispersed nature. This meant using a great deal of motor transport to move arriving and departing aircrews from one section to another on the airfield whilst they were being 'processed' through the system.

Meanwhile, on the RAF side, 125 Squadron left for Hurn in March 1944 in preperation for the Allied landings in Normandy. The squadron was replaced by No.157 from Predannack — the last fighter squadron to be based at Valley, as it turned out. Defensive patrols were carried out in the Irish Sea area but the main objective was to re-equip with Mosquitos fitted with Mk.X AI. To train aircrew in the use of this latest airborne radar a Wellington was used. By early May the squadron became operational and left for Swannington in Norfolk.

The question of Valley's transfer to Transport Command arose once again in 1944 by which time its use as a transatlantic terminal had grown enormously. Headquarters, Air Defence of Great Britain (which Fighter Command became in November 1943) had to concede that the interests of the station were now predominantly transport and that, furthermore, the American presence was the major factor in its continued existence. In a memo written at the end of January 1944 the Air Office Administration said:-

"About eight months ago it was submitted to C. in C. that it would be in the interests of all concerned if R.A.F. Station, Valley, were transferred from Fighter to Transport Command.

The C. in C. would not then approve. The war situation has, however, altered considerably in the interval, and Transport Command claims that the use of Valley has increased. ADGB Units at Valley are as follows:-

One Night Fighter Squadron

One Air Sea Rescue Squadron

Under the new ASR organisation our commitment at Valley will be concluded. Six night fighter squadrons are being transferred to 85 (Base) Group so that it would appear that the permanent basing of a Night Fighter Squadron at Valley is also problematical. SASO agrees with this view.

The organisation and administration of Valley has for a long time provided difficulties. By far the biggest interest there is that of Transport Command, for whom major Works Services to the value of £425,000 are being undertaken in the development of a trans-Atlantic base.

It seems only logical, if operational considerations permit, that

50

Valley, with these major Works and Establishment interests should be handed over to Transport Command, this Command being allowed to retain facilities for one T. E. Squadron on a lodger basis."

The senior air staff officer agreed with this view pointing out that in his opinion, "It becomes a question of whether it is worth our while to carry the administrative burden." He continued, in a memo to the C. in C., "Dealing with the affairs of the Station causes us a considerable amount of work. . .for which we get little operational return. In view of this, I recommend that we should offer the Station to Transport Command. . ."

The C. in C. was in agreement and by March a number of changes had been worked out, which included:- transfer of Valley to 44 Group, Transport Command to take effect from 18th March 1944, retention of a fighter squadron, (125 Sqdn), as a lodger unit for the time being, retention of GCI Trewan Sands under the operational control of No.9 Group, Woodvale Sector, and transfer of responsibility for 275 ASR Squadron to Coastal Command, with effect from 15th April under Woodvale's control until the squadron's expected move to Warmwell, which took place in May. It was the end of Valley as a Fighter Station.

One person who took a keen interest in these changes was Lady Megan Lloyd George, MP for Anglesey (and daughter of Lloyd George). She was of the opinion that Valley's success as a transatlantic terminal for American bombers offered some exciting prospects for post-war civil aviation in North Wales. In June 1944 she met W. P. Hildred, Director General of Civil Aviation, at the airfield and discussed its potential as a bad weather diversional alternative to London Airport. Lady Megan stressed the advantage of this arrangement, obviously with local interests very much in mind whilst Hildred, more circumspectly, pointed to the need for runways of 5,000 yards length and the problem this might present at Valley. Lady Megan, clearly, could do nothing further at this point but once the war ended she was soon putting forward her case with enthusiastic support from the County Council.

Reference has already been made to the daily internal shuttle flights through Valley. In addition to these a daily C-54 (the military version of the DC4 commercial airliner) flight began to operate from the US and other North Atlantic bases from May onwards.

Often VIPs were carried, as on 9th June, when the Chiefs of Staff of the US Army, Air Force and Navy flew into Valley. Many of the passengers travelling in the opposite direction were 'war weary' operational crews returning to the United States for a rest.

In July this shuttle was replaced by an Army Ferrying Division operation codenamed 'Snowball' which again used C-54s shuttling from Presque Isle, Main, along the northern Atlantic route to Britain. A great deal of cargo was carried on these flights, which was offloaded at Valley for transporting to ultimate destinations. The C-54s then flew to Prestwick with local passengers and cargo for that base where they picked up loads for the return flight overseas. In July sixty 'Snowball' aircraft arrived, a figure which became the average for the coming months.

Shuttle and cargo operations were on a 24-hour basis at Valley, dealt with by crews on a 12 hour shift system. In addition to the 'Snowball' flights during this period (August 1944) the internal shuttle consisted of two daily scheduled flights — southbound from Nutts Corner and Prestwick arriving at Valley at 11.35 hours and departing at 11.55 hours whilst a northbound flight from Hendon arrived at 14.35 hours and departed at 14.55 hours. From September 1944 Valley became a request stop only and from then on the C-47s would not land unless requested to do so on the previous day.

The American unit also had its own aircraft — three in fact, a B-17G serial 43-39065 plus a couple of hacks, and Airspeed Oxford named 'Little Winston' and a Cessna Bobcat, serial 43-31824.

The vast majority of American aircraft that came to Valley had genuine aircrew and authorised personnel on board, but it was not always so. A Liberator which flew in from Marrakech in March 1944 proved to have some unexpected occupants — two stowaways described in the unit's record as, "British soldiers possessing a strong homing instinct."

Another surprise was provided by a UC64 "Norseman" which landed on 30th June. Its arrival is recorded as follows — "at 15.55 hours, after careering about the airfield a C64 flew over the control tower, touched down on grass, crossed one of the runways not in use and finally stopped on the grass. This unusual arrival was reported to the US office who found the aircraft was being flown by an American private who had stolen it from Wharton and was, in his own words, "headed for France", but had been forced into Valley by bad weather elsewhere. The only glory he was going to achieve was to be put into the guardroom by the US Provost Marshall!"

But the station commander had slightly more worrying problems during this period, one of the main ones being low morale amongst RAF personnel because of the strong USAAF presence. He wrote. . . "morale would improve if British aircraft could either be stationed at Valley for some purpose or if larger numbers of RAF aircraft could be directed from overseas. . .the lack of RAF traffic is generally disappointing."

Not only was there a lack of traffic but a steady decline in RAF strength also. A comparison of RAF and USAAF numbers shows the extent of change over 12 months:-

Station Strength	Sept.1943	Oct.1944
RAF Officers	110	41
N.C.O.s	130	51
Other ranks	1216	496
USAAF Officers	31	52
N.C.O.s	41	579
Enlisted men	288	579

i.e. a 58% reduction in RAF numbers and 75% increase in those of the USAAF.

In addition 85 civilians had been recruited locally to work in the American unit, mostly as cooks, cleaners, drivers etc. They were paid by the Ministry of Labour and earned an average of £3 per week. Civilian employment in the Enlisted Mens Mess, for instance, was sufficient to reduce by 50% the number of Americans on duty although the Mess Officer, Lt. E. McKamey remarked (unofficially) that it took three civilians to equal the efficiency of one of his men — a classic example of military bias against civilians!

Meanwhile, the flow of American aircraft continued unabated. In August 1944 353 four-engined aircraft and 144 twin-engined aircraft arrived. As many as 99 B-17s and B-24s landed from Meeks Field on 16th September, and there would often be equal numbers departing for Warton, Burtonwood or other bases in England. The monthly figures for transiting crews during September was 1,588 officers, and 2,332 men, all received, processed, fed, billeted and sent on to operational units, together with 11,814 pieces of baggage. Also some 500 'Happy Warriors', officers and men who had come to the end of an operational tour of duty, were flown home to the United States for a rest, and some 79,000 lbs of incoming mail was received and sent to delivery points throughout the UK and Europe. Such was the scale of activity at Valley.

Accommodation, in one way or another, had always been a problem for the Americans. For instance, when dealing with transient aircrews the problems of transportation, information and billet assigning had been numerous because such facilities were dispersed throughout the airfield but a number of building programmes had been put in hand during 1944 to try and improve the situation. Included in this scheme was the 'Services Centre', a long building on Site 7 designed to bring together a number of services for transient aircrews.

In September the following sections moved in from dispersed sites — Navigation, Weather, Medical, Intelligence, 8th Air Force Debriefing, Transient Services, Billeting, In-flight lunches and Information.

Another important building project was the Terminal Building, designed to be the main centre for dealing with American traffic. It was nearing completion in September 1944 and was opened in October. The Americans were not too impressed however, as the unit record notes, "The new Terminal Building had been long awaited by all personnel at Valley and although still not completed it is now housing several sections of our activities and also several RAF functions. The building was constructed by the British and will be used jointly both by the RAF and AAF. Construction was painfully slow and the actual design and facilities appear to have been poorly planned."

"The one natural advantage that its completion will affect is the consolidation of sections previously scattered in separate buildings and Nissen huts." This building later came to be used as the SHQ in post war years until replaced in the late 1970s by a more modern structure.

An increased RAF commitment, albeit on a small scale, came in November 1944 when 1528 BAT (Beam Approach Training) Flight formed. Its purpose was to provide practical training for pilots in the use of blind approach systems. The unit had six Oxfords, two Link Trainers, ten flying instructors and an intake of 13 pupils every ten days. Training commenced in December although technical shortcomings and unserviceability of radio equipment caused difficulties, making it impossible to keep to intended schedules.

Immediately before Christmas one of the (very infrequent) accidents involving American aircraft occurred, when B-24 42-51232 was lost in the sea off Holyhead on 22nd December. It was from the 36th Bomb Squadron based at Cheddington, and on that day was one of three B-24s diverted, after returning from a radio jamming mission over Europe, because of bad weather.

By the time the aircraft was approaching Valley the weather there was bad also, with visibility at 1,800 yards and low cloud down to 500 feet. The B-24's pilot called the tower to say that he was, "On top at 4,000 feet and had 2½ hours of fuel on board". Unfortunately he had badly miscalculated and in fact had only enough fuel for another twenty minutes of flying. To make matters worse the pilot announced that the aircraft's 'G' Box (a navigational aid) had become inoperative and that he had no information on the local radio range facility, the use of which would have greatly assisted him in locating Valley. Whilst still attempting to find the airfield the B-24's engines stopped after the fuel tanks ran dry. The crew were then ordered to bale out. At 5.45 p.m. the local Coast Guard reported having seen the aircraft crash into the water near Holyhead Mountain. By 7.15 p.m. two crew members had been found, the pilot near Holyhead and the co-pilot near Trearddur Bay but of the remaining eight crew members there was no trace. After questioning of the two survivors it appeared that the others had parachuted into the Irish Sea without flotation gear and had perished.

At the subsequent investigation the pilot was criticized for misreading the fuel state of his aircraft. It also turned out that because of inadequate briefing he had no knowledge whatsoever of the local radio range, nor did he know of the position of the nearby mountains in relation to the airfield. Sadly, at the time the pilot gave the order to bale out, he did not even know Valley was situated on the coast of an island and the resultant probability, therefore, of his fellow crew members landing in the sea.

During 1945 American bombers still continued to arrive in large numbers although the year got off to a poor start when heavy snowfalls in January drastically reduced activity for long periods. The number of aircraft handled fell by 50% from 266 in December 1944 to 148.

In February, when the wintry weather still restricted operations the level of activity nevertheless increased considerably. The unit record states, "Despite the fact that the field was dead for eleven days, (because of heavy snowfall), Valley managed to handle 384 tactical arrivals, or more than twice January's total. When ATC and transient aircraft arrivals are included the figure becomes 471 as compared with 245 in January."

The record continues, "It is worth re-stating at this point that the prompt dispatching of sizeable aircraft movements calls for more than good weather and enough crews.

"Well planned parking and servicing can save many a precious hour of flying time and Valley strives constantly to save those hours; 8th and 15th Air Force ships are kept on separate strips and each night Operations is furnished with a mimeographed plan of the field showing the locations of each ship. Earliest tactical arrivals are dispatched first and are usually in the row nearest the taxi-strip."

"On February 1st there were still 32 tactical aircraft remaining from the January backlog, most of them having been on the field since January 19th due to the record snowfall. By February 3rd all had departed."

"By the end of the month two War Weary Liberators had arrived at Valley, the vanguard of what promises to be a considerable movement. The crews (for the flight to the US) will consist of Pilot, Co-pilot, Engineer, Radio Operator, chosen from War Weary combat personnel, plus ATC navigator."

The Americans were taking no chances with the aircraft and, "As each War Weary arrives from the Base Air Depot it receives an immediate and thorough inspection. This includes a fuel consumption test and a careful check of all emergency eguipment."

The record continues, "While the Berlin-bound flow of tactical aircraft continued to glisten on Valley's parking ramps and a few drab 'War-Wearies' began to appear the base personnel situation reached a point which almost paralleled the aircraft movements. Rotation of eligible Enlisted Men to the United States for additional training and re-assignment finally began in earnest and, as the month was drawing to a close the long anticipated WAC detachment arrived, sending morale up quite a few degrees."

"While the physical change was immediately noticeable, especially in the improved appearance of the male personnel, base activity hummed smoothly on without interruption . . ."

In March, with the European war in its final stages, the flow of American aircraft continued unabated, with a record total of 518 for the month. During April this torrent subsided and the figure for that month was down to 194 aircraft.

On 20th April the last sizeable movement took place when 60 aircraft landed and the final curtain was rung down on 9th May, V-E Day plus one, with the arrival of eight 10th Air Force Liberators, the very last to land being Liberator 442305, flown by Flight Officer S. Carter. Since July 1943 Valley had handled over 5,000 American aircraft — 2,734 B-17s, 1,869 B-24s, 271 C-47s and 174 other types, bringing the grand total to 5,048 aircraft.

When the war in Europe ended so did the work of the 8th and 9th Air Forces but Japan had still to be defeated and so the plan was to withdraw the Air Force back to the United States from where re-deployment would take place to the Far East in order to continue the fight against the Japanese.

Not unexpectedly Valley was to play a major role in the re-deployment which was planned at ATC H.Q. and code named 'White Project'. Headquarters had promised the American unit a period of one month to rest and prepare for the start of White Project but it began barely ten days after VE day.

Thus almost before the base had a chance to gain any respite the flow of aircraft started once again but this time in the reverse direction. There was little chance to formulate a definite, over-all plan and: "As a result improvisation was the rule, and Valley was certainly a base which could improvise, having had almost two years experience", to quote the unit records.

White Project was to have two phases — Phase I covering the departure of four engined aircraft and Phase II for twin engined aircraft.

The first aircraft, a Liberator which had never seen operational use, landed on 17th May and from then on an average of 62 aircraft arrived daily. Inevitably the airfield was nicknamed 'Happy Valley' by homeward bound crews.

Generally the procedure was for aircraft to arrive from British bases in the morning or early afternoon and after an overnight stay by aircrews, departure would be early next morning to make room for the next batch of aircraft. Nearly all departing aircraft had some 20 or so men on board — 9 or 10 airmen, the rest being ground crews or passengers.

Re-deployment called for schedules that would permit aircrews to be briefed and processed in a minimum of time. To begin with the daily timetable was:- two briefings each morning, one at 0600 hours and the other at 0800 dealing with a total of 62 crews on average. A route briefing was given first, followed by a weather briefing, then pilot and navigator would report to the briefing dispatch section, the co-pilot would go to the Engineering section to pick up the aircraft's papers whilst the radio operator would remain for further briefing on radio procedure.

In Briefing Dispatch pilot and navigator received and checked the flight plan. Fuel consumption was calculated and the crew would then have their clearance papers signed. The next step was Operations before going out to the aircraft and starting the long but welcome journey back to the United States.

Meeks Field, Iceland, was the first scheduled stop for these aircraft, with Lagens in the Azores as an alternative when the weather was bad at Meeks. The ultimate destination of four engined aircraft sent via the northern route was Bradley Field, Connecticut.

The first westward movement took place on 20th May when 72 aircraft departed. On the following day 61 left for Meeks, to be replaced by a similar number of aircraft from UK bases. Following arrival in the USA aircraft were either prepared for further service in the Pacific or put into storage ready for disposal as surplus. Crews were given thirty days leave for, "rehabilitation, recovery, and recuperation", as the official description put it, before preparing for tours of duty in the Far East. But the dropping of atom bombs on Horishima and Nagasaki finally ended the Pacific War and the aircrews were no longer needed.

Naturally enough there was great haste to get home and not every aircraft that left Valley was fully serviceable although each was supposed to have been thoroughly inspected. Perhaps the most remarkable case was that of Liberator 44-10528 of the 446th Bomb Group, which upon arrival in the US was deemed unsafe and written off!

By June the pressure to get home had built up considerably and the daily quota of aircraft handled was increased by 25 from 62 to 87. It was decided that the best way of coping with the extra aircraft was by overlapping departures and after some tests to prove that the new schedules would work the daily quota was stepped up from 9th June. The original and revised schedules can be summarised thus:-

0330	0600	0800	1100	1300
I	I	I	I	I
0600	0800	1100	1300	1600
62 overnight crews wake and have breakfast	Briefing, two sessions to handle crowd	Aircraft dispatched	Field empty	62 New aircraft arrive

Original Re-deployment schedule

0430	0700	0800	0900	1300	1700
I	I	I	I	I	I
0700	0900	0900	1200	1600	1900
62 overnight crews wake and have breakfast	Briefing	25 new aircraft arrive and are parked in a separate part of the airfield	62 overnight aircraft dispatched	62 new aircraft arrive. 25 crews who arrived in the morning are briefed	25 morning arrivals are dispatched

Revised Schedule

Another aspect of White Project was the huge demand for fuel. Previously, it had varied from 12,000 to 15,000 gallons per day, with aircraft carrying out short internal flights within the UK only but now, with heavy bombers setting out on much longer flights, demand shot up to 50,000 gallons per day. It was found impossible to maintain adequate stocks and so train loads of extra fuel had to be stored in sidings one mile from the airfield and drawn directly into bowsers which used a hastily constructed dirt road to reach the airfield.

The peak day was 19th June when 154 aircraft arrived and 64 were dispatched. That day's arrivals included B-17 497280 of the 385th Bomb Group, landing with faulty hydraulics which as a result sent it headlong off the runway to become the first and only casualty up to that date.

Although the aircraft was damaged beyond repair its crew sustained only minor injuries. Whilst it was the only re-deployment aircraft under Valley's control which was lost at the base another loss occurred in June when Liberator No.11-0018 of the 446th Bomb Group ditched en route to Lagens because of engine trouble. Rafts were seen in the vicinity of the ditching, but ships at the scene could find none of the nine man crew or six passengers.

Probably the worst accident was that to B-17 44-6005 of the 351st Bomb Group, which crashed near Cader Idris on 8th June whilst flying from Polebrook to Valley. Twenty men were killed. In July, Liberator 41-29369 departed for Meeks Field but crashed in Skye with the loss of fourteen lives, and in August 21 A26s arrived from France, one of which crashed on landing after suffering engine failure. It was destroyed by fire.

The most difficult part of White Project, i.e. the dispatch of four-engined aircraft was over by mid July, when the last remnants of the 8th Air Force Bombardment Groups departed, the very last being a B-24 of the 44th Bomb Group, flown by 1st Lt. Gene Williams. From then on until the end of the month, unpredictable weather and leisurely arrivals of 9th Air Force twin-engined transport aircraft under Phase II of White Project gave a much needed breather.

As a result the American unit was able to take stock of its property, much of which was being prepared for shipment to the United States, or return to the RAF.

For the twin engined aircraft, C-46s, C-47s and C-53s, good weather was more important than for the heavier aircraft. Flying conditions, especially winds, had to be favourable before they could be dispatched to Iceland. Diversions to the Azores were not feasible for these aircraft and in fact the C-46s (Curtiss Commandos) which began to arrive in mid July were all routed to Iceland via Prestwick, where fuel tanks were topped up in order to assure the maximum fuel load for the flight.

Unlike the cavernous tanks of the Fortresses and Liberators which allowed them to fly to Iceland and return if necessary, the fuel tanks of the Commandos permitted a one way flight only. The C-47s (Dakotas), however, could safely be sent directly to Meeks Field without a re-fuelling stop at Prestwick.

Along with the increase in twin engined aircraft activity came a reduction in the number of men departing on each aircraft. In place of the 20 man quota for Fortresses and Liberators the C-46s carried 15 men on average and the C-47s 10 men.

Although a good third of late July departures were still four-engined aircraft (including a movement of 34 Navy PB4Ys and almost 100 B-17/B-24s which had been interned in Sweden and Switzerland), the average load of these aircraft was likewise only fifteen men.

From 20th May until 10th July, the last day of exclusive four-engined aircraft departures a total of 1,956 Fortresses and Liberators had been handled — a daily average of 37 aircraft. During the same period 60,284 men were billeted, an average of 1,116 per day, which meant good business for the PX if nothing else! When twin-engined operations started the daily averages dropped to 18 aircraft dispatched and 790 transiting men handled.

By the end of August the exodus was over and White Project completed — some 2,500 aircraft and their crews had returned to the USA.

Many of the GIs who operated the American base at Valley had also departed and their sections closed. It had been a difficult time, in a sense, for the officers of the unit. Beset by problems such as woefully inadequate accommodation, many of the sections not up to strength and too many men with incorrect skills for the job assigned to them, the officers nevertheless managed to lead the unit successfully, enabling it to fulfil its alloted task.

The unit's record closes with the statement, "On 31st July 1945, with the Base's mission all but accomplished, the Commanding Officer could rest assuredly on his laurels completely convinced that the policy of operating with a minimum of personnel who have a maximum of initiative is bound to get results".

Then with its work at an end, the 1407th AAF Base Unit finally disbanded and left in September. There remained only a handful of Americans to operate the radio section and provide a small servicing facility for any possible US diversions.

With the American unit having departed, what of the RAF? Very little of any significance was taking place, the only activity being that of 1528 BAT Flight. They were joined by a detachment of Sea Otters (the updated version of the Walrus) from 281 Squadron in March, but they found themselves with little to do. The detachment left for Northern Ireland in October whilst 1528 Flight's establishment of aircraft grew to eight Oxfords. In addition, the unit changed its title from 'BAT' to 'RAT' (Radio Aids Training Flight). Its job now, was to teach American Radio Range let-down techniques to Transport Command pilots but it was a short lived commitment as the Flight left for Blakehill Farm, Oxford, in December.

On 15th September the airfield, like many others, was thrown open to the public in commemoration of the Battle of Britain. For this, the first

'Open Day' of many, seven thousand people came to see aircraft types such as the Mustang, Typhoon, Anson, Oxford, Beaufighter, Stirling, Dakota, Spitfire, Hurricane, Wellington, Lancaster and Mosquito amongst others.

By the autumn of 1945 activity had almost ceased completely and the station had reached the nadir of its existence. October and November were the quietest months ever.

Thus Valley's wartime history came to an end. The few years since its establishment in 1940 had seen remarkable changes: where previously there had been nothing but sand dunes there now stood a large airfield and transatlantic terminal which had handled thousands of heavy bombers during its life.

The airfield had become the most important in Gwynedd, if not in North Wales, and had served two main purposes. Firstly, to combat the threat of enemy attack from the west, during the darkest days of the war, and secondly, as a terminal for USAAF aircraft crossing the Atlantic. It was the only airfield of the eight in Gwynedd to be substantially developed. In the course of that development many problems had arisen, ranging from windblown sand damaging precious aero engines to inadequate domestic accommodation. Dealing with, and attempting to provide solutions to these problems provided many headaches for the administrators but in the main all difficulties were successfully resolved.

However, it is not the everyday burdens of administrators which grip the imagination when thinking of Valley during those momentous years, but rather the sight, in one's mind, of Spitfires and Hurricanes, and the roar of their Merlin engines as they patrolled the skies of North Wales; the dark shapes of Beaufighters taking off into the night; aircraft manoeuvring on the bleak airfield on cold, grey winter days, and the contrast of the brilliant light of summer if the sun was shining.

Perhaps the most impressive and rousing spectacle of all would have been provided by the American heavy bombers, with rows of mighty Fortresses and Liberators lined up on hardstandings, the uncamouflaged metal of their fuselages reflecting something of the light, whilst others flew overhead, the noise of their engines thundering around the airfield as they joined or departed the circuit.

These are the images which best encapsulate Valley's wartime history and which will forever be associated with it.

Chapter 4

Aircrew Training & Army Co-operation
R.A.F. Mona & R.A.F. Bodorgan

Mona is the only airfield in Gwynedd to have been used in both World Wars and as such has the longest history, although that history is not continuous, the site having been used for other purposes between 1919 and 1940.

The main use was that of the old RNAS airship station accommodation huts as a small isolation hospital, known as the Druid after a nearby farm. By 1940 the huts, positioned as they were in a rather bleak and exposed spot, had deteriorated to such an extent that their useful life was over. New buildings were urgently needed but disagreement arose over a site between the Welsh Board of Health and the local hospital Committee — the former wanted a new site in or near Llangefni whilst the latter thought the hospital should remain where it was.

Discussions were still continuing when the Air Ministry stepped in and resolved the argument by announcing in September 1941 its intention to construct an airfield on the old airship station, and therefore the land would have to be requisitioned for this purpose.

The Hospital Committee, however, managed to score quite a success by extracting an agreement from the Ministry that the Druid Hospital would be re-established in new buildings near Llangefni — with all costs to be met from Air Ministry funds. The hospital was opened in March 1943.

Not so fortunate were ten families living in adjacent farms to the airship station, who lost their homes and land to make room for the new airfield. They petitioned their M.P., Lady Megan Lloyd George, but she, in the circumstances of the war emergency was powerless to prevent their eviction. One family in particular suffered a double loss when a 21 year old daughter died at the very time their home was being demolished. When workers employed on the airfield's construction heard of this tragedy they organised a collection and presented the bereaved family with a substantial sum of money.

Construction work continued apace throughout most of 1942, enabling the RAF in December to occupy its seventh and last airfield in Gwynedd during the war. This airfield was to be known as Mona, the old Roman name for the locality — a short simple name, likely to cause little confusion within the RAF and easy to pronounce in comparison with other local place names which could have been used, e.g. Gwalchmai,

Bodffordd, Heneglwys or Llangefni. Difficulties which had arisen over the naming of Valley and Bodorgan proved that a straightforward name which caused no difficulty in pronunciation by the average Englishman was best in this part of the country. In Mona's case the RAF got it right first time and none of the problems of lost equipment and personnel experienced in the early days of the other two airfields arose.

The usual triangle of runways had been constructed, the longest extending to 1,800 yards and the other two of 1,100 yards length. Airfield lighting was of the Drem Mk.II type and three T.1 hangars were built. Later, when aircraft left in the open began to suffer from the effects of bad weather, as many as seventeen Blister hangars were added to provide the necessary shelter.

Mona came under control of No.25 (Armament) Group, Flying Training Command, with a station commander of Group Captain rank. The original intention was to form an air gunners school here, to be known as No.6 AGS, with a proposed establishment of 34 Ansons and 27 Martinets catering for a trainee population of 240.

However, Flying Training Command decided instead to transfer an already existing gunnery school, No.3 AGS, then based at RAF Castle Kennedy to Mona. Accordingly, a collection of more or less obsolete aircraft, mostly Bothas relegated from operations to training, arrived at Mona during December. Between the 8th and the 24th, forty eight Bothas were transferred from castle Kennedy plus six Battles, eight Martinets and two Ansons.

Training commenced on 3rd January 1943 with forty pupils from No.2 Signals School who made up No.1 Wop/Air Gunners Course.

On the following day the unit experienced its first accident at Mona when Martinet HP134 swung violently on landing, careered off the runway and struck a pile of stones which had been left alongside the runway by civilian contractors engaged on airfield construction.

The pilot, Pilot Officer E. P. Thomas, who was unhurt in the accident was an interesting and somewhat unusual character. He was the son of an extremely wealthy Nigerian dignitary, and was believed to be the only Nigerian flying with the RAF at the time. His skin was as dark as it could possibly be, earning him his nickname at Mona — "23.59"! This was a reference to the 24 hour clock used in the Services, 23.59 being one minute to midnight of course, and the darkest part of the night. Thomas was an engaging and attractive personality, well liked and popular with his colleagues, and was exceptionally religious. Normally courteous and gentlemanly, he would let himself go at social events such as Mess parties after being persuaded to take a few drinks and would demonstrate wild

African dances in a most impressive manner. Undoubtedly his personal qualities were of the highest order but the same could not be said of Thomas's flying. He had a tendency to be involved in mishaps and accidents rather more frequently than one would have expected. It was rumoured that whenever he 'bent' an aircraft his father would always foot the bill. On 11th February the Ministry of Information Colonial Film Unit arrived at Mona to take some shots of Pilot Office Thomas in action for eventual inclusion in a propaganda film to be shown in the colonies.

On the same day the first passing out parade was held when No.1 Course members were presented with their chevrons and badges by the station commander, Group Captain Bearne.

At the same time, No.5 (P) AFU Special Flight came to Mona by air and road from Tern Hill. This Flight, equipped with Miles Masters, consisted of twelve Turkish Officer pupils, a liaison officer plus maintenance and instructional staff. The latter's task was to impart the techniques of air gunnery then in use within the RAF to the Turks.

During the war Turkey was, of course, neutral and whenever groups came to the Allied side for training an equal number had to attend similar courses organised by the Axis powers, in order to maintain neutrality.

The Turks that came to Mona were, by all accounts, handsome, good looking men but volatile and quick to take offence. One even threatened to kill a staff pilot after misinterpreting an innocent remark as an insult. Their training ended after five weeks and they departed on 11th March 1943. Later, in September and October some Czech and French pupils were taught and in 1944 a number of Belgians and Norwegians also undertook training at Mona.

During this period in the station's history, training courses lasted for seven weeks with an average of sixty pupils per course. Air firing exercises were carried out in Bothas, and later Ansons, firing at drogue targets towed by Martinets. On the ground another part of the pupils' training was the rather unusual activity of clay pigeon shooting using 12 bore shotguns. As rapid response and quickness of the eye was important for an air gunner it was thought that shooting at clay pigeons helped to develop these qualities, and furthermore it had the advantage of being very inexpensive in comparison to aerial firing practice.

To the country sports and shooting types amongst 3 AGS's staff it was rather galling to see enormous quantities of 12 bore cartridges used by the RAF in this manner when they themselves could not obtain their usual supplies because of the war, especially when the countryside surrounding Mona was teeming with game. Sometimes the Armaments Officer could be persuaded to part with a box of cartridges by promising him a brace of pheasants!

Two of the station's Bothas were involved in accidents during February 1943. The first, W5029, crashed on landing, on the 15th as did the second aircraft, W5024, on the 28th. Luckily no casualties resulted from either crash. Both aircraft were flown by Polish pilots. In fact quite a few Poles flew as staff pilots with 3 AGS. They were well aware of the Botha's notorious lack of power, and it was said, being Catholic they would cross themselves just before taking off.

Another of 3 AGS's aircraft, Martinet HP219, suffered a mishap in February when its engine cut following mismanagement of the fuel system by the pilot. The engine could not be re-started and so the pilot decided to carry out a wheels up landing in a field near Aber which resulted in some damage to the aircraft's tailplane.

Curiously enough, two other Martinets suffered similar fates during this period, on consecutive dates. The first was Martinet HP623 from 61OTU, which force landed on Prestatyn beach after its engine failed as a result of incorrect operation of the fuel control levers by the pilot. This accident occurred on 3rd April. Then on the 4th Martinet HP267 of 1486 Gunnery Flight, RAF Valley force landed on Cymyran Beach adjoining the airfield, slightly injuring the crew. As in the other cases engine malfunction came about through the pilot's failure to change fuel tanks correctly.

Bodorgan had also experienced a similar situation when Martinet HN889 of 1606 Flight force landed at Craig Farm, Anglesey, in February, with the pilot again being blamed for negligence in his management of the aircraft's fuel system.

Meanwhile at Mona, from May 1943 onwards the unpopular and seriously underpowered Bothas began to disappear as they were replaced by Ansons, which proved a good workhorse for the rest of the war, as they did throughout the RAF in general of course. Easy to fly and without any vices, the Anson's nickname 'Faithful Annie' or just 'Annie' was a good indication of the aircraft's qualities.

Also during May a slightly different type of training from the usual was embarked upon, when thirty one airwomen were posted to the station for preliminary training as Flight Mechanics on re-mustering from Balloon Operators.

Pilot Officer Thomas, previously mentioned, had an interesting time during May when he was again well to the forefront on the publicity side. On the 23rd, which was Empire Day, the BBC broadcasted a talk given by him immediately after the 9.00 p.m. news. The talk was entitled "Civis Romanus Sum" which can be translated as "I am a Roman citizen". It refers to an ancient Roman law and judging by this, Thomas's talk probably had as its subject matter some aspect of the law.

On 29th May, whilst the CO, Group Captain Bearne was at Holyhead delivering a 'Wings for Victory' speech Thomas was delivering a similar speech at Menai Bridge and Benllech, having been promoted to Flying Officer after his Empire Day broadcast. However, his time in Anglesey soon ended when he was posted to Squires Gate, Blackpool, in June.

Throughout the rest of the summer and into autumn training continued normally at Mona, with, for instance, an output of sixty pupils from No.26 Course in September. As it so happened this proved to be the penultimate course instructed by staff of No.3 AGS because in October news was received that the unit was returning to Castle Kennedy at the end of the month.

On the 29th ten Ansons and ten Martinets left Mona, to be followed in November by the remaining aircraft — thirteen Ansons, fifteen Martinets, one Master and one Tutor.

At Mona, SHQ staff remained as the nucleus of the station's next unit — No.8 (Observers) Advanced Flying Unit which was to form on 15th November. It was in fact the last unit of its type formed during the war. The purpose of such units was to extend the usefulness of Observers by training them in other aircrew duties such as radio operation, air gunnery, navigation and bomb aiming. Ansons were the only aircraft flown, forty one at first, intended for a pupil population of 180 split into three categories: navigators, bomb aimers and wireless operators/air gunners with sixty trainees in each group.

In January 1944 Air Ministry approval was given for this figure to be increased to two hundred trainees and an extra four aircraft, bringing the total to forty five Ansons.

Two of these aircraft were damaged beyond repair on 25th January when a severe gale struck camp resulting in the collapse of two Blister hangars in which the aircraft were housed.

Another Anson was lost on the 29th when it crashed at Llanerchymedd, killing the pilot and seriously injuring three other men. On 16th February a fourth aircraft was destroyed after crashing between Conwy and Llandudno, killing all five crew members on board.

Usually training lasted for ten weeks or so for each course at Mona. For those training to be bomb aimers practice targets were located on a small range at Lligwy Bay on the north east coast of Anglesey.

On this range two observation quadrants to plot hits and misses were in use, operated by ten airmen with a sergeant in charge — all billeted in local houses.

They had to deal with a workload of eight or so aircraft per day using the range. The left hand quadrant had a gun emplacement adjacent to it, in which two Browning machine guns were located. Once a week a group of trainee air gunners from Mona would arrive by lorry and would fire these guns at targets placed out to sea.

The sergeant in charge of this small range met, courted and eventually married a local girl and now, some forty years on, he still lives (in retirement) quite close to Lligwy, in the village of Moelfre.

Some physical remains of the range existed until recent times. The left hand quadrant was more or less intact though the gun emplacement was in a ruined state. During the late 1980s these buildings were demolished and all traces eradicated. The right hand quadrant had met a similar fate many years previously.

Another practice target was Conwy Bridge, to which an infra-red device had been attached. This system allowed practice bombing of pinpoint targets in an urban area and worked by projecting an infra-red beam along a previously decided line and angle necessary to score a hit. Aircraft bombsights had linked photographic plates sensitive to the infra-red end of the spectrum and, assuming the attacking aircraft was on the correct course, when the bomb release button was pressed an image would be recorded on these plates.

Back at Mona the plates would then be developed to reveal whether a hit had been achieved on the bridge, or as one staff pilot said, "To see by how much the pupil had missed."

Sometimes ranges further afield were used such as Wharton Sands in Morecombe Bay. Mona's record book shows that on 29th October Anson MG808 dropped a practice bomb on RAF Cark in error for the Wharton Sands range! No damage resulted but an embarrassed crew no doubt earned a black mark.

Navigation pupils learnt morse, radio procedures and the techniques of navigating by dead reckoning. The main training area was North Wales and the Irish Sea with coast-hugging trips down to South Wales also a prominent feature of training. After successful completion of their courses pupils were sent to OTUs.

Many of the staff pilots were highly experienced and often 'resting' from operational tours of duty. They sometimes had to work hard, especially when training continued throughout periods of bad weather in order not to disrupt the all important flow of trained aircrew into OTUs and ultimately, operational squadrons.

During bad weather, errors by trainee navigators in particular, had to be watched for carefully and an over-dependence on their advice could lead to some hazardous situations.

A certain amount of stress could creep into the job and sometimes it would be necessary to let off a bit of steam. One of the favourite methods, already referred to in Chapter 1, was flying under the two bridges that span the Menai Straits. One pilot recalls that he used to delight in carrying out this manoeuvre particularly if he had a pupil on board who was asleep (it was common practice, if there was room available, for pupils to join training flights not to receive instruction but merely to build up flying hours and many would use the time in order to gain some extra sleep). At the critical moment the pupil would be rudely awakened from his slumbers and the shock of seeing the aircraft skimming the waves of the Menai Straits as the bridge loomed directly ahead would, more often than not, cause a moment of panic, to the merriment of the rest of the crew!

Reference has already been made to the operation of Valley as a transatlantic terminal for USAAF bombers, and as Mona was only six miles away it sometimes happened that American pilots confused the two airfields and landed at Mona by mistake. For instance, on 14th March a Liberator inward bound from Marrakesh landed and in April three Dakotas, followed by a C54 Skymaster (the military version of the DC4 commercial airliner) made the same mistake.

Probably more would have been caught out except for the advice of Mona's Flying Control Officer at that time — C. H. Leonard. Well known in the world of male voice choirs within Wales he recalls that whenever an American 'heavy' threatened to land he would inform its pilot in no uncertain terms to, "Keep going for another two minutes," knowing that the pilot would then see Valley and realise his error.

In January 1944 target-towing Martinets from Bodorgan took up temporary residence, due to the unserviceable condition of their own grass field. Later that year they were forced to use Valley for the same reason.

Another target-towing commitment began in April 1944 when a small detachment from 776 Squadron RNAS arrived at Mona. Consisting of two Blackburn Skuas and a handful of Navy personnel, the task was to provide target-towing facilities for gunnery practice by naval MTBs based at Holyhead.

Training continued uninterrupted at the airfield until the end of the war with the same unit, No.8 (O) AFU, still in residence. Flying ended officially on 19th May 1945. Three days before this date a fatal accident occurred when Anson N9911 from Llandwrog crashed a few hundred yards from the airfield whilst attempting a night landing, killing the pilot and two others. It was the last wartime accident at Mona. Disbandment of the unit came on 14th June.

The final entry in the record book reads:- "Flying Officer C. Hughes granted special leave to take part in the General Election as Labour candidate for Anglesey."

The officer referred to was Cledwyn Hughes from Holyhead who, at the end of the war, was Mona's Station Adjutant. He failed to win the Anglesey seat from Lady Megan Lloyd George in 1945 but vanquished her in 1950. Thereafter he pursued an extremely successful career, becoming one of Wales' most respected politicians, and now as Lord Cledwyn of Penrhos, leads the Opposition in the House of Lords.

After No.8 (O) AFU had been disbanded Mona went on a Care and Maintenance basis until its future could be decided. One member of the C. & M. party still resides locally and recalls that it was a particularly pleasant time for him and others in the party. Regardless of rank everyone lived in the Officers Mess, in some comfort and with plenty of good food to eat. At the time of disbandment 45 Ansons remained and one of the final tasks was to ferry them to MUs for disposal. Responsibility for despatch of the aircraft lay with the C. & M. party who craftily used every delaying tactic possible, thereby prolonging their own relaxed stay by several weeks!

When deliberating over the airfield's future, the Post War Airfield Requirements Committee foresaw that the runways near the A5 main road would have to be curtailed and the road itself controlled or diverted if aircraft were to use Mona in peacetime. The thresholds of all three runways at their southern ends were dangerously close to the road, and whilst this did not matter so much in wartime with relatively little traffic to worry about, the situation could be very different if post war road traffic grew appreciably, which indeed it did.

After a few years of lying dormant the airfield came into use again in the early 1950s as a Relief Landing Ground for Valley. It was not necessary to maintain three runways and so the two short ones were closed whilst the main runway was lengthened at its northern end.

Mona continues to this day in the humble but very useful role of RLG and since the mid 1970s it has also been the home of Mona Flying Club, a flourishing civilian club which has successfully established itself here.

R.A.F. Bodorgan
Of the three wartime airfields in Anglesey, Bodorgan was the smallest and least important. Situated in a rather remote backwater, it had a grass field only, with no runways ever envisaged and its main task was the unglamorous job of army co-operation, providing aerial targets in the form of pilotless drones for Royal Artillery gunners at the nearby camp of Tŷ Croes.

Nothing of any major significance ever took place here and the station had no vital operational role to fulfil yet its story is not a dull and lifeless one. The flying of pilotless target drones was not entirely without interest.

The story began in June 1939 when Air Ministry officials arrived in the small village of Hermon in south west Anglesey to survey a site for the new airfield. Following a previous aerial survey an area of agricultural land was chosen, one mile from Hermon and close to Bodorgan Hall, home of Sir George Meyrick, owner of extensive estates in Anglesey and elsewhere. Naturally enough Sir George resented the fact that an airfield was to be located within a stones throw of his home and being a man of some considerable influence he persuaded the Air Ministry to seek alternative areas.

His agent spent two days during mid-August touring the island with a Ministry official diligently searching for other sites. They found two — one at Cwyrtai some three miles further inland and the other at Cemlyn on the north west side of Anglesey. However, this was something of an academic exercise because there was no real possibility whatsoever that the Air Ministry would agree to use either site. Bodorgan had been earmarked for the airfield and Sir George's agent was realistic enough to observe, "They will take Bodorgan because it will be cheaper and quicker to utilise than the others".

Further advantages included the coastal location, distance from large populations and lastly, Bodorgan's proximity to the army camp at Tŷ Croes.

But without precise information coming from the Air Ministry or RAF as to the exact use to be made of Bodorgan rumours spread locally that the bombing school (No.9 BGS) then at Penrhos was to be the occupier of the airfield. To quote Sir George's agent once more, "The bombing school may come from Llŷn due to a lot of accidents."

"They say it was a mistake ever having a bombing school there near the mountains." He may well have been right of course about locating an aircrew training school so close to mountains but No.9 BGS remained at Penrhos — with war having just broken out the RAF needed bomb aimers and air gunners as never before.

In December 1939 the necessary land was requisitioned and construction began of the airfield. It was another example of the boost given to Anglesey's economy by wartime construction projects.

Whatever one's views about the morality of war with its waste and destructiveness, it invariably offers economic opportunity and profit to some, whether individuals, groups or geographical regions. Such was the case with Gwynedd, which saw a number of military building projects taking place in addition to the influx of manufacturers such as Saunders-Roe, Hunting Aviation and Daimler, for example, into the area. There was no doubting the benefit this activity brought to the local economy.

Many workers could earn high wages for the first time in their lives whilst engaged upon airfield construction and other similar schemes. One of the Bodorgan estate employees, for instance, abandoned his 35 shillings (£1.75) per week gardener's job to work on the airfield and was delighted to earn £3.10.0d (£3.50) on his first day. Admittedly, he recalled, it was a Sunday and he had to endure a scolding from his wife for working on the Sabbath but nevertheless. . .!

There is another story told of a Llangefni man who, having heard that work was plentiful and highly paid went to Bodorgan hoping to find employment. By then construction was well advanced and the RAF already in occupation. He went up to the guardroom at the main gate and announced in Welsh — "Dwi wedi dwad yma i chwilio am waith, dwi yn dallt fod yna ddigon i gael yma", (I have come to look for work, there's plenty here I understand).

Taking no chances with anyone that spoke a foreign language the RAF guards promptly arrested him and refused to release the unfortunate man until he could convince them he was a bona-fide Welshman!

The airfield, when completed, consisted of a relatively small grass landing area 1,000 yards by 1,000 yards by 960 yards with two Bellman hangars plus one Blister. There was no flying control building as such, only a small watch office which performed this duty.

On 11th September 1940 'Z' Flight of No.1 AACU arrived from Watchet to take up its duties followed by 'J' Flight from Penrhos a few months later in January 1941. The aircraft operated by these flights were Queen Bees — radio controlled and pilotless variants of the well known Tiger Moth developed especially as target drones for live gunnery practice. Later 'J' Flight re-equipped with Hawker Henleys, Tiger Moths and Martinets.

The other unit at Bodorgan was No.2 Maintenance Flight which became 3506 AAC Servicing Flight in December 1943; it serviced the Henleys at Bodorgan plus those of other flights based elsewhere. All three units belonged to No.1 AACU. Eventually Bodorgan came under the control of No.70 Group in December 1941.

Before any flying began part of the airfield was obstructed in case of invasion. No sooner had this been done than an Anson from Squires Gate chose the exact spot to make a forced landing!

At first the official name was Aberffraw but as the months passed it became clear that it was unsuitable. Constant delays of mail, mis-postings of airmen, lost consignments of equipment sent by rail etc. were ended by renaming the airfield RAF Bodorgan on 15th May 1941. Local residents, however, referred to it as Penrhynhalan, and still do.

On 2nd December 1940 the first pilotless flight by a Queen Bee at Bodorgan took place. It remained under control for 2½ hours but crashed on landing. In fact landing remained the most difficult part of Queen Bee operation as in piloted flying. After the ground based operator brought his aircraft down to 15 feet, a trailing line connected to the magneto would touch the ground, causing earthing and thus stopping the engine. The Queen Bee would then land of its own accord.

The operator's control panel was fairly simple, consisting of a face with three buttons marked: 'left', 'straight' and 'right'. Diagonally across the face were four marked: 'climb', 'level', 'glide' and 'dive'. Radio equipment in the Queen Bee received control signals and transferred them into movements of the rudder, elevators and ailerons. This airborne radio equipment was prone to failure particularly after near misses by artillery fire and the aircraft would then become uncontrollable and either crash or head out to sea on a pre-determined course flown automatically after such failure.

Soon after Queen Bee operation had begun at Bodorgan it became evident that the area was subject to 'difficult' winds especially when coming from the sea. After P4801 crashed from a height of three hundred feet in February 1941 an instruction was issued — "In view of the peculiarities of local weather pilotless flights will be restricted to those days on which conditions are not approaching the borderline for a safe approach."

Another problem which arose during the summer of 1941 was a series of losses caused by battery failure. Following the loss of P5738 on 20th August when it sank off Tŷ Croes, every battery used in a Queen Bee had to be subjected to a vibration test and undergo one hours flight under ground control conditions but with a safety pilot on board. However, V4788 crashed at Glantraeth, Anglesey in September, again from battery failure, and after this accident every aircraft had to be fitted with two batteries in parallel.

Early in 1941 No.48 MU at Hawarden needed extra space to disperse aircraft and so some fields adjacent to Bodorgan were requistioned and prepared as No.15 SLG (Satellite Landing Ground). These fields, between Bodorgan Hall and the airfield, were surrounded by woodland, requiring a 120 foot wide swathe to be cut in order to provide a passage between the two areas — SLG and airfield. Aircraft were not crammed into every available corner of the SLG however, so as not to provide an irresistible target in the event of an attack. A maximum of thirty or so aircraft were usually stored at any one time.

The first arrived on 1st April 1941 — five Lysanders, followed by Hurricanes and later, Wellingtons. By the end of May thirty aircraft were dispersed, literally, only a few hundred yards from the back door of Bodorgan Hall. During the summer part of the building itself was requisitioned as accommodation for officers and nearby buildings for airmen.

One problem which worried the station commander, Squadron Leader B. Robinson, was the lack of proper airfield defence, caused mostly by insufficient manpower. He wrote in May, after some additional airmen had been posted in, "After eight months endeavour to create Station Defences without the men, an intensive training and field works programme will soon be possible. Of the two manning exercises held this month the Station Defence Force was defeated by the enemy (Royal Irish Fusiliers from Trearddur Bay) on both occasions."

In June a practice invasion alert was staged. With army reinforcements and the local Home Guard acting as the enemy, three Blenheims flew from Penrhos to carry out mock low level dive bombing.

Another large scale invasion exercise was carried out on 20th July during which to quote the official record, "Flight Lieutenant Holroyd and Squadron Leader Robinson dive bombed the camp in a bastard formation of one Henley and one Hurricane." Interestingly enough the record states, "The Hurricane did not show up so fast against the Henley."

A few days later Sq. Ldr. Robinson again took part in a similar exercise when he flew a Lysander accompanied by one of 'J' Flight's Henleys in order to carry out a mock attack on the Menai Bridge for the benefit of the Home Guard, whose duty it was to defend this important link between Anglesey and the mainland.

To digress for a moment, there is a story told of two Anglesey farmers returning home by car from Bangor after an evening's drinking, who were stopped by a Home Guard sentry at the entrance to the bridge. After beckoning the driver (who relates the story) to open his car window the sentry rudely thrust his rifle inside, started to wave it about and asked the occupants for their names and addresses. However, from his slurred speech and odd manner, it was apparent to the two men, not entirely sober themselves, that their interrogator was also under the influence of drink! Being in a jovial state of mind they exchanged understanding glances and without a word being spoken the rifle was snatched from the sentry's grasp and the car sped off, its occupants roaring with laughter. They paused momentarily half way across the bridge to throw the gun into the water, 150 feet below, before heading for Anglesey, leaving behind a rather befuddled sentry, no doubt wondering how he was going to explain to his superiors the loss of his rifle!

The local Home Guard also feature prominently in another delightful story concerning an airfield defence exercise held at Bodorgan during the night of 12/13th June 1943.

It had been decided that a test of station defences would be a good thing, and so, for this purpose the Malltraeth and Aberffraw units of the Home Guard were to assume the role of invading German paratroops who had been dropped three miles north of the airfield in order to carry out an attack upon it. This prospect, given the Home Guard's reputation, was regarded with some hilarity at Bodorgan, where the outcome of the 'invasion' was looked upon as a foregone conclusion.

The 'attack' began at dusk on the 12th when RAF patrols were sent out, but as the station record states, "there was little to report." However, the Home Guard were busy and by 4.30 a.m. had penetrated to the airfield's boundary, without being seen, and had broken through near the hangars and wireless station. After various skirmishes during which certain points were captured, including the CO's office, it was said, 'fighting' ended at 7.30 a.m. and breakfast was served, with the attackers celebrating an undoubted victory.

But how had they achieved their success? Dismissed as ineffectual amateurs they had, nevertheless, managed to outwit better trained and equipped men. Was there something radically wrong with the defences of Bodorgan perhaps, some fatal weakness or deficiency that would quickly deliver the airfield into the hands of the enemy in the event of a real invasion? The CO and his officers need not have worried because the men of the Home Guard later revealed they possessed an unfair advantage.

Many, in the ancient tradition of country dwellers, were poachers of the local squire's game and they had intimate knowledge of every field, wood, copse, ditch and lane on the Bodorgan estate. Long experience of giving the slip to Sir George Meyrick's gamekeepers had made them expert in the art of silent and unobserved movement!

Mention has already been made of the fact that 'rogue' Queen Bees, hit by gunfire and not responding to control, were designed to fly out to sea until they crashed. Usually this was the case but not always. On 24th February 1942 V4793 was hit by artillery fire and as a result refused to respond to control signals. Incorrectly, as it turned out, the operating crew assumed their charge had taken a seaward heading to a watery grave and promptly forgot about the aircraft.

In fact the Queen Bee's automatically programmed response to control loss, i.e. to fly a heading out to sea had also failed and as a result this machine continued to fly in a southerly direction until it eventually crashed on the slopes of Snowdon.

The impact and subsequent fire had been witnessed by residents of Rhyd Ddu in the valley below, who informed the police. At this stage the aircraft type was not known to the rescue party which set off for the southern side of the mountain under the mistaken impression that the crashed aircraft was piloted. It was a perfectly reasonable assumption to make of course, but a fruitless search in poor weather revealed not the slightest sign of any pilot/s either dead or alive, forcing a baffled rescue party to retreat and ponder upon the mystery! The incident has an element of humour but the authorities should have been informed of the runaway Queen Bee, thereby saving much wasted effort.

Some confusion over pilotless aircraft also arose on 9th May 1942 when the Duke of Kent visited Bodorgan. His stay was brief but nevertheless there was time to give him a demonstration of the skills needed to fly radio controlled drones.

As Queen Bee L5896 was being put through its paces in front of the Duke, the station hack, a Tiger Moth, came in to land but was suddenly caught by one of Bodorgan's freak crosswinds and overturned. Luckily damage was minimal and the pilot unhurt though extremely embarrassed after losing control of his aircraft in the Duke's presence.

His Royal Highness, watching this unfortunate mishap, turned to an NCO standing nearby and said, "Wasn't that a Queen Bee?" The NCO, who was in fact Flight Sergeant J. Shelby-James, in charge of the Henley ground crew, replied, "No Sir, it's a Tiger Moth and there's a pilot in it." Outwardly the two aircraft types were similar and impossible to tell apart from a distance. At this moment the Queen Bee came in to make a perfect landing on the opposite side of the airfield. "Is there a pilot in that one?" enquired the Duke.

"No Sir, it's a Queen Bee."

"Pity there aren't more aircraft flying without pilots!" said a somewhat bemused Duke. Tragically, he was killed three months later in a flying accident in Scotland.

In October 1942 'J' and 'Z' Flights became 1606 and 1620 Flights respectively. No.1620 remained with Queen Bees but 1606 re-equipped with Hawker Henleys, Tiger Moths and Miles Martinets, for target towing duties.

Target towing could be a tedious job and to relieve the boredom pilots would sometimes indulge in low flying by 'beating up' gun positions. This had its dangers as exemplified by the loss of Henley L3301 in September 1942 when it collided with a 3.7 A.A. gun at Tŷ Croes. The aircraft crashed into the sea and no trace of the crew was found until five months later when some of the pilot's clothing was washed up on a nearby beach.

A similar accident occurred on 11th February 1944 to a Martinet at Holyhead. The operations record states, "Martinet HP183. . .provided co-operation for Bofors Guns at 1,000 feet with 2,000 feet of tow. Co-operation was successful. At 11.15 the aircraft flew over the gun park, losing height. The starboard wing struck a gun, the aircraft turned upside down, crashed, and skidded for 300 yards. The pilot was killed and crewman slightly injured. No technical defects — unauthorised low flying."

Three days later another Martinet was engaged on army co-operation three miles west of Valley when a Mosquito, approaching from the sea, collided with the drogue towing cable despite a red flare being fired by the Martinet pilot. The Mosquito lost nearly seven feet from its starboard wing in the collision but it was successfully landed at Valley — a tribute to its flying qualities.

The drogue ended up in the sea probably, but when drogues were lost over land, either through failure of the towing cable or destruction by gunfire, people living in the surrounding countryside would eagerly collect every scrap. Women in particular prized the material for household use and many houses had curtains etc. made from drogues.

In December 1943 following re-organisation of AAC resources within 70 Group, 1620 Flight left Bodorgan whilst 1606 remained, with eight target-towing aircraft and one Tiger Moth.

Co-operation took place not only with Tŷ Croes but also other gun emplacements in the region — at Penrhyn Mawr, Gorsgoch near Holyhead and the Coastal Artillery Practice Camp at Llandudno, for example. A summary of flying for the month of February 1944 shows:-

Tŷ Croes 4th HAAPC	— co-operation given – 71.15 hours
CAS Llandudno	— co-operation given – 17.45 hours
533 & 534 Battery	— co-operation given – 5.15 hours
44 Battery	— co-operation given – 2.15 hours
5th Cheshires	— co-operation given – 2.00 hours
Defence Course, Bodorgan	— co-operation given – .30 hours

The 'Defence Course' referred to was one regularly organised by No.70 Group to give RAF officers and NCOs some knowledge of command in the field, army style, during an emergency. The first course assembled in

July 1943 and the last in May 1945. Training was given in fieldcraft, use of weapons etc. and with so much variety of ground near Bodorgan it was an excellent place for such courses to be held.

The station commander, Squadron Leader P. ap Ellis came within a hairsbreadth of losing his life on 12th April 1944 when his Tiger Moth crashed near Bodedern during a local cross country flight. Both he and his passenger, an airman, received injuries which put them on the dangerously ill list for a few days, but neither died, fortunately.

Also in June army co-operation was a little unusual because it involved radar and experiments with strips of aluminium foil known as 'window'. This foil was capable of producing false echoes on a radar screen and could be used to create the electronic equivalent of a smoke screen. The aircraft dropped quantities of 'window' and then flew through it whilst radar operators at Tŷ Croes attempted to distinguish between aircraft and 'window' as presented on their screens. The purpose of the experiment was to determine the effectiveness of this metal chaff as a weapon against radar controlled anti-aircraft guns, and the outcome was described as "completely successful" in the station's record book under the heading 'Most Secret'. All details of radar were, of course, kept secret throughout the war.

Meanwhile, No.48 MU was busily ferrying aircraft, Wellingtons in particular, in and out of the airfield. The MU's own pilots carried out this work usually although squadron pilots had been used at the start of the operation. Many found Bodorgan's small grass field difficult and following some mishaps it was decided that aircraft should return to 48 MU first before delivery to squadrons. During the latter years of the war frequent waterlogging of the airfield in winter forced temporary cessation of the operation.

This recurring problem affected Bodorgan's other residents also. In October 1944 for instance, conditions became so bad because of prolonged wet weather that the airfield had to be closed and operations transferred to Valley. Three Martinets were to be used and a Bellman hangar, office, and small store made available. The unit took its own fuel to Valley and transport was laid on for crews to and from the airfield each day. Bodorgan became unserviceable again during the last week of November.

By then some changes were taking place including the arrival of two other army co-operation units — 650 Squadron and a detachment of 577 Squadron. The aircraft flown were Martinets and later, Hurricanes, used specifically for gun laying practice.

The other change, heralding Bodorgan's eventual fate was the closure, on 30th December, of 48 MU's SLG as by then it was no longer necessary to disperse aircraft. In December 1944 650 Squadron took over all commitments, operating from Valley. Thereafter activity remained at a fairly low ebb until the war ended. On 26th June 1945 650 Squadron disbanded, whilst 3506 Servicing Unit had left for Weston Zoyland, in Somerset, on the previous day. In July No.70 Group disbanded and Bodorgan came under the control of No.12 Group. The airfield was closed to all traffic from 23rd August 1945 and went on a Care & Maintenance basis in October.

Bodorgan's closure was felt with considerable regret by many of the local population because in its few years of existence the station had become something of a centre for social life in the area with frequent dances and parties being organised. This brought a welcome stimulus to the lives of many living in the nearby villages of Aberffraw, Hermon and Malltraeth.

No peacetime use could be found for the airfield and so the Air Ministry relinquished its hold on the land which then reverted back to agriculture, no doubt much to the relief of Sir George Meyrick and Bodorgan Estate tenants. The buildings were, for a period, used to house Italian POWs, who had been set to work on local farms, causing the heart of more than one farmer's daughter to beat faster in the process!

In July 1946 the Air Training Corps' Welsh Wing sought permission to use the airfield as a base for No.63 Gliding School, which since 1943 had been operating from an unsatisfactory site at Tal-y-Cafn near Conwy. The School provided gliding experience for North Wales cadets but the flying ground had power lines and the Conwy river in close proximity.

No doubt the ATC saw an opportunity to gain an improved site. They carefully pointed out that flying would be at weekends only and would not interfere with agriculture but the answer from Sir George was an emphatic "no". After five years of having an airfield adjacent to the family home he wanted nothing more to do with aviation of any kind. It was a disappointing but understandable reaction.

Of all the wartime airfields in Gwynedd, Bodorgan is the least changed by the passage of time. It still remains very much as it was in 1945 and although the hangars have been demolished most of the buildings are standing. Indeed, many are in everyday use, housing light industry and the Bodorgan Estate offices. The grass airfield is easily distinguishable as no re-hedging took place. Surrounding woodland and fields, where so many Wellingtons and other aircraft were stored, are exactly as they were forty five years ago.

Chapter 5

Training to be an Air Gunner
R.A.F. Llandwrog

Like most of Gwynedd's other airfields Llandwrog was built on a coastal
site. At the southern end of the Menai Straits a small flat peninsula,
known as Morfa Dinlle, extends from the coastline, and it was this
peninsula which the Air Ministry deemed suitable for another airfield
site. A defensive fort — Fort Belan — had already been built here in the
Napoleonic era. Now, in the dark days of 1940 this spit of land was again
being put to use as part of Britain's fight against another European enemy.

Construction began in September 1940 and proceeded at a rapid pace.
Although located in an area where coastal sand dunes existed, very much
like Valley, the site of this latest airfield, in contrast, did not require
anything like the amount of levelling needed to construct it and none of
the problems of wind-blown sand arose. The usual triangle of tarmac
runways were built, each 150 feet wide, the longest being 03/21 at 3,100
feet, the shortest was 32/14 at 2,990 feet and the third, 09/27 was 3,000
feet long. Hangars were built on the northern side of the airfield and
consisted of two T1s, a Bellman and seven Blisters, none of which are
extant. Airfield lighting was the Drem Mk.II type.

Llandwrog was the nearest settlement and so, following the usual
practice, the airfield took its name from this small village.

Originally it seems that Llandwrog was to be a fighter station, a
rearward base in the event of an invasion of southern England or
conversely, a forward base should any invasion come from Ireland — a
possibility discussed by Hitler and the German High Command in
December 1940.

The airfield's importance in this respect was reinforced by the
provision of strong defences. Large numbers of mines were placed around
the boundary and along Dinas Dinlle beach, in addition to many machine
gun posts sited at key points. Pillboxes were built in considerable
numbers and preparations were made for a large RAF Regiment unit to be
based here.

In the event, however, threats of invasion receded and Llandwrog
became, rather more mundanely, a training station. Flying Training
Command took over on 1st July 1941, the station coming under the
control of No.25 Group.

Wing Commander Bruce, station commander at Penrhos, relinquished his post at the beginning of July and moved northwards to take command of Llandwrog. Then a few days later No.9 Air Gunnery School took up residence, equipped with twelve Whitleys and a similar number of Lysanders. The Whitleys were Mark I, II, III, IV and Vs which had seen front-line service during the early part of the war, had then been relegated to OTUs and were now being handed down, in a somewhat battered state, to Air Gunnery Schools. The main difference between the various Marks as far as the training of air gunners was concerned lay in the type of turret installed — Marks I, II and III had manually operated turrets whilst Marks IV and V possessed powered ones.

Training began almost immediately when 46 members of Course No.1 assembled in mid July for a six week course. Forty one successfully completed their training at the end of August after which they proceeded to OTUs and were now being handed down, in a somewhat battered state, Bomber Command. It was a pattern repeated for all subsequent courses. The most promising men on any particular course, about one or two, would be offered commissions whilst the failures, again just a few, would be withdrawn and re-mustered to a more suitable form of training.

In order to carry out the aerial part of their training the u/t air gunners, five or six at a time, would fly in a Whitley, each taking turns to fire at drogue targets towed by Lysanders up and down Caernarfon Bay. The aircraft would fly about a mile or so out to sea with the Lysanders always on the seaward side of course, flying parallel to the Whitleys at a distance of one to two hundred yards.

Use was also made of the airfield that summer for night flying exercises by Oxfords from No.11 SFTS, RAF Shawbury, where the grass field could not withstand the heavy demands of constant flying. The Oxfords would leave every evening for Llandwrog and return the following morning.

In fact the first fatal accident at Llandwrog involved one of these aircraft when Oxford T3933 crashed into the sea immediately after taking off during the early hours of 21st July. The 30 year old pilot, described as one of the School's most promising pupils, had only night flying exercises to complete before obtaining his wings. His body was discovered three weeks later trapped underneath a raft moored in the Menai Straits near Caernarfon. The school lost another Oxford on 3rd August when it flew into cloud obscured hills above the Sychnant Pass near Conwy.

More serious, indeed the worst accident ever to take place at any of Gwynedd's airfields during the war, was the one that occurred at Llandwrog on 10th October 1941 when two Whitleys collided in mid-air resulting in the death of seventeen men. During the afternoon of that day Squadron Leader Barker, OC Flying, took off in K7252 with six gunnery

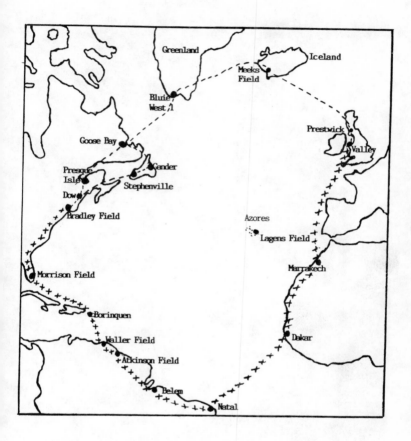

------- Northern Route

+ + + + + + + Southern Route

Airfields used by American aircraft flying to and from
the USAAF base at RAF Valley

An aerial photograph of Valley taken from a Spitfire of 542 Squadron on 13 August, 1945, over 100 aircraft are on the airfield, including B-17s, B-24s, B-26s and C-47s (Photo: D. Watkins)

Pilots of 247 Squadron (Photo: Imperial War Museum)

*Line up of Spitfires of 350 (Belgian) Squadron, formed at Valley in 1941
(Photo: Imperial War Museum)*

A B-24 lands at Valley during World War II (Photo: USAAF)

*Corporal D. Stewart and Master Sergeant L. McPherson carry out
maintenance work on a B-24 at Valley (Photo: USAAF)*

A B-24 about to depart from Valley on its homeward journey to the United States witnessed by three RAF Officers in a posed photograph (Photo: USAAF)

An example of the B-17 flying fortress, hundreds of which used the Transatlantic Terminal at Valley from 1943 onwards. This particular aircraft has been photographed on an actual raid over Germany in October 1943 (Photo: Imperial War Museum)

The Chapel Hall at Caergeiliog,
once used as the operations room for RAF Valley

remains of the 'Q' site at Newborough Warren

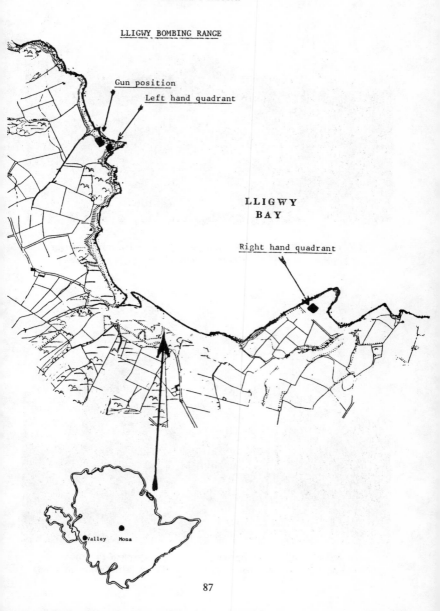

LLIGWY BOMBING RANGE

Gun position

Left hand quadrant

LLIGWY
BAY

Right hand quadrant

Valley Mona

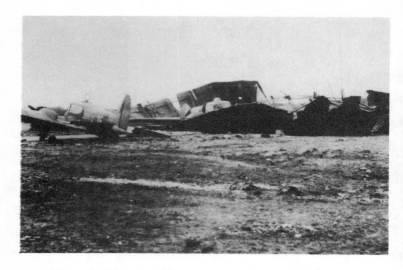

*Aftermath of the gale of 25 January 1943 — a collapsed Hangar
and damaged aircraft (Photo: Public Record Office, London)*

*Remains of Lligwy bombing range photographed in 1986.
On the left are the gun butts and on the right, the observation quadrant*

One of Mona's buildings still standing in the 1990s
— the Wireless Telegraphy Station, now used as a cattle shed

Mona as it looked from the air in 1987

RAF Bodorgan photographed from the air during World War II. Fourteen Wellingtons are parked around the field surrounded by woodland

An aerial view of Bodorgan in July 1987 showing the technical site, little changed from wartime days

Wartime buildings still in use at Bodorgan in 1990

Llandwrog photographed in July 1987

*Derelict Control Tower at Llandwrog
just prior to rebuilding and modernisation*

The Mountain Rescue Team in the hills, November 1943 (Photo: A. Evans)

*Flight Lieutenant Graham, originator of the RAF's
Mountain Rescue Organisation (Photo: A. Evans)*

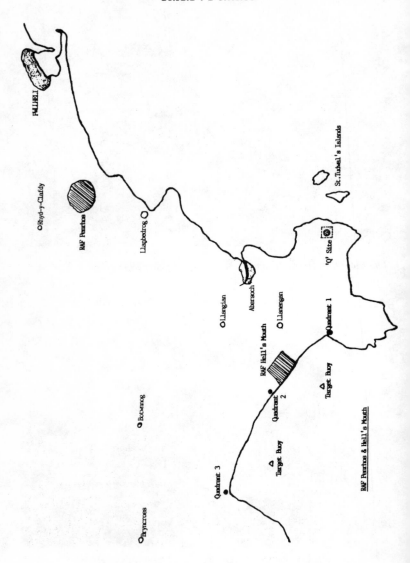

PWLHELI

○Rhyd-y-Clafdy

RAF Penrhos

○ Llanbedrog

St. Tudwal's Islands

'Q' Site

Abersoch

○ Llangian

○ Llanengan

Quadrant 1

RAF Hell's Mouth

○ Botwnnog

Target Buoy

Quadrant 2

Target Buoy

Quadrant 3

○ Rhyncroes

Target Buoy

RAF Penrhos & Hell's Mouth

Hurricanes of 312 Squadron at Penrhos during the winter of 1940/41
(Photo: Zdenek Hurt)

Wreckage of Hurricane P3612 which crashed on take off
at Penrhos on 22 February 1941

Penrhos in 1986

Plaque erected at Penrhos by Plaid Cymru in September 1986 to commemorate the burning of the Airfield by Welsh Nationalists in 1936

pupils, their instructor and a civilian engineer on board. Five minutes later a second Whitley, K9041, took off also with six pupils and an instructor on board. Training continued normally for an hour, then Squadron Leader Barker's aircraft returned to the circuit and proceeded to land on runway 09/27. As it happened, the other Whitley also returned within a minute or so of the first but came in directly to its final approach on the same runway from a steep turn to port without doing a circuit. The two pilots did not see each other until it was too late to avoid a collision. Both machines crashed to the ground and burst into flames. All seventeen men died in the blazing wreckage.

One witness was Flight Lieutenant M. Holmes, the officer in charge of the target towing flight. He reported what he had seen: "At 15.15 hours I had just landed on the east-west runway and was standing in my Lysander aircraft ready to get out when I saw two Whitley aircraft coming in to land. I had seen Sqn.Ldr. Barker make a wide circuit of the aerodrome and he was making a long low approach in the yellow Whitley.

"I saw the black Whitley (K9041) make an approach on the aerodrome without doing a circuit. The pilot was turning to port all the time and Sqn.Ldr. Barker was below him, on his starboard. When K9041 levelled out at about 200 feet it was almost immediately below the other aircraft. I think the pilot saw Sqn.Ldr. Barker's aircraft then for the first time, slightly above him. The pilot tried to avoid a collision by turning away to port, but his starboard airscrew cut Sqn.Ldr. Barker's tailplane off. Sqn.Ldr. Barker's aircraft turned on its back and went straight into the ground, bursting into flames on impact. The tailplane fell about fifty yards away from the main crash. It was impossible to get near the blazing wreckage.

"After the impact with Sqn.Ldr. Barker's aircraft the black Whitley began to swing to port, dropping its starboard wing, hitting the ground just at the commencement of what looked like a spin, and burst into flames on impact. In my opinion the failure of the pilot of the black Whitley to make a circuit was the cause of the crash, and therefore he was guilty of an error of judgement."

The accident was witnessed at close quarters by another Llandwrog pilot, Pilot Officer W. Adams, who was standing a few hundred yards from the runway on which the aircraft were landing. After describing the crash in a similar fashion to Fl.Lt. Holmes he gave this account of Whitley K9041's final moments. . ."I could see that his starboard wing was damaged and sagging and both motors were opened full out. He was losing height in his right hand turn and was obviously going to crash, and I went towards the point where he would crash. At the time of impact I was about fifty yards away. The starboard wing hit first, the machine went on its back and the tail came off, and the machine burst into flames. I got to within ten yards of the aircraft, downwind, but as my face was singeing I had to get back."

Following this accident the station commander had an encounter with a rather angry local policeman annoyed at not being informed of the crash, having heard about it only through rumours in Llandwrog village on the day after the event. In company with another policeman, for moral support, he went to the airfield and demanded an interview with the CO. The request was granted and the CO was told that it was his duty to inform the police of any fatal accidents, as they were the agents of H.M. Coroner and it was the law of the land that they be so informed.

But Wing Commander Bruce was not in a conciliatory frame of mind. Tempers flared though everyone behaved with restraint. The CO, distressed at having lost so many men, including his OC Flying, replied that he was too busy writing to next-of-kin and the Air Ministry to bother about the police. Furthermore he said it was an internal matter for the RAF only! This episode illustrates well some of the tension between RAF and civil authorities over the matter of reporting fatal flying accidents, which, locally, had risen to an unprecedented number.

Llandwrog's Whitleys and Lysanders were joined by six Ansons in January 1942, when they arrived from Penrhos to form a permanent night flying detachment, bringing with them responsibility for the air gunnery commitment which Penrhos was relinquishing.

By this time over two hundred men had been trained as Air Gunners here and had gone on to the RAF's 'sharp end' in Bomber Command, but what was the experience really like? What kind of life did the trainee Air Gunners lead during their few weeks at Llandwrog? Was it generally hard and uncomfortable with many privations, or not?

One man who undertook training here during early 1942 was Leslie Sidwell. Although over thirty years of age and considerably older than most aircrew, Sidwell nevertheless had a strong desire to get into the air and see some action. His account of his experiences at Llandwrog provides an excellent impression of life on the station. He writes:-

"I was in a party of about fifty men who had remustered from ground jobs to become U/T Air Gunners at a time when the training of AGs was being lengthened on the lines of pilot and navigator training. Instead of the old course, just on guns, we were first put through an eight weeks course at No.14 ITW, Hastings, where we studied subjects such as RAF law and administration. . .Eventually we were posted to Llandwrog to form No.8 Course of six weeks — later extended to ten weeks".

Sidwell found himself at Bangor railway station just after midnight on 2nd January with the group, and as he was in charge he telephoned Llandwrog to inform them of the situation. . ."When I phoned to say we were stuck at Bangor they said they weren't expecting us. However, not only did they send out transport for us immediately, but when we arrived — cold, wet, and very hungry — they had a good hot meal awaiting us. We slept until noon and in daylight saw where we were billetted — almost on the beach: we had heard the sea roaring away in the darkness but sleep had come quickly. When we saw our position, the little huts were only some twenty yards away from a pebbly beach, which was wired off and big warning signs stood every twenty yards which proclaimed in English and Welsh:

DEATH! HEAVILY MINED!

It shook us to think that we had slept so close to this mined beach. The huts were just for sleeping, no water, heating, lighting, or toilets. We had to go to the Communal Site early morning, every day, taking our kit with us. Ablutions, toilets, dining hall etc. were all at this site, and we returned to our huts each night to sleep, or try to.

"When we went up to the Communal Site on our first day, we found that an invasion exercise was in progress. The Army and Home Guard were trying to 'take' the aerodrome — successfully it seemed, with khaki uniforms pouring over the runways in triumph. But our irascible CO (Wing Commander Bruce) had completely refused to acknowledge the validity of such an exercise, he was only concerned with making up lost flying time, through bad weather, and we saw him rush out of his office waving his fists and yelling, "Get off my bloody runways you idiots!" We enjoyed such lighter moments."

"The weather was appalling during the first part of our stay, especially January. Huge gales raged, with rain, sleet, snow and frosts alternating. Snow inside the camp did not settle much but roads outside were blocked. We had much rain and floods. Our huts leaked badly and were often awash with water, and very cold indeed. Sleep was out of the question and the noise of the roaring sea on the pebbles was never ending.

"There were four old buses, still bearing the insignia 'Liverpool Corporation' on their sides, that were supposed to transport men from outlying sites to the Communal Site during early morning. But they were such clapped-out old bangers that they kept breaking down while the weather worsened and they were a joke, to the annoyance of Liverpudlians amongst us, who disliked their fair city's name being involved in such a shambles. We rose at 6.00 a.m. and a corporal would take us for PT just outside our huts, in darkness, with floods all around us, in biting winds and rain or sleet — the most bizarre PT situation I ever experienced.

"Then we would hurriedly dress, grab our things for the day and be ready for the bus at 6.40 a.m. but we learnt to cut out the long cold waits by footing it up to the Communal Site for ablutions and breakfast.

"Towards the end of January we were cut off for a few days by snow blocking the roads; no mail or papers. Flying was even more badly held up. If the wind let up briefly and visibility temporarily improved, things would change rapidly. Brief spells had to be seized and we waited in the crewroom a lot, hoping for better weather forecasts. Flying days were supposed to alternate with classroom days but things had to be changed to suit the cirumstances."

"I personally had an odd affection for the old Whitleys that we flew in, having seen them flying pre-war, in that nose-down position, from where they were built, near my Coventry home.

"I was in a Mk V (N1475) on January 25th when first one engine cut out at sea and then the other. I was in the pilot's cabin at that moment, and as there was no intercom, he sent me back through the narrow tunnel in the wing spar to alert the rest of the crew. Through the pilot's skill we just made a landfall at Morfa Nefyn for a successful belly landing. It was Sunday midday and the owners of the nearby Linksway hotel put on a fine meal for us before transport arrived."

The aircraft suffered Cat. B damage.

"Our flying training consisted of twenty hours of air-to-air firing exercises while stooging along the coastline of Caernarfon Bay, the pupils in each Whitley taking it in turn to climb into the turrets and fire two hundred rounds at the drogue towed by the accompanying Lysander. We also shot film using a cine-gun. Many setbacks occurred — engines failing, Lysanders not turning up, guns and turrets going u/s, drogues being shot away and weather butting in".

"Back on the ground an oasis of warmth in the cold and wet for some of us was a farm on the airfield boundary known as 'Rhydfelen', where Mrs Williams lived. She was a hospitable sort and we had some smashing ham and eggs in her cosy parlour, out of the gales."

So did many, many others like Les Sidwell. Throughout the war Mrs Williams provided food and warmth for any airman that went to Rhydfelen and many friendships were made. After the war quite a number of those who experienced her hospitality kept in touch and visited regularly. She took great pleasure from seeing her 'Old Boys' again.

What of the Air Gunner syllabus? Sidwell writes; "Bags of theoretical and practical classroom work to learn the workings of Browning and V.G.O. guns inside out, stripping and clearing of stoppages, operation of various turrets, their theory, mounting guns in them and re-arming, theory of the reflector ringsight, harmonising them with guns, bullet trail in various positions, gravity drop, aircraft recognition, over one hundred types to recognise from all angles, types of ammunition in use, e.g. ball, tracer, incendiary, explosive, armour piercing etc. and pyrotechnics."

"We had to pass mid-term and final examinations in all subjects, including scoring the required number of hits on drogues during flying exercises. Those failing to attain a pass rate of 60% would get the dreaded R.T.U. — i.e. thrown out with the ignominy of being Returned To Unit."

"We were supposed to visit RAF Penrhos twice weekly in order to practice on their panoramic turrets, then on, after lunch, to Hell's Mouth, where we fired from ground turrets at moving targets rigged up seawards on the great deserted stretch of sands there. We loved that but our old Liverpool buses struggled to get there and visits were consequently few. We had to load up all our own guns and ammunition to take with us on such trips. It was a fifty mile round trip and the many breakdowns caused us to know a cafe in Pwllheli quite well!

We also did some firing from fixed ground turrets at Llandwrog, on the far perimeter, usually on afternoons in biting sleet or rain with freezing hands to clear gun stoppages."

On 23rd January 1942 No.8 Course and everyone else at Llandwrog had a big surprise when shortly after mid-day, with low clouds reducing visibility, a lone JU88 suddenly appeared through the murk and proceeded to fly at high speed across the airfield, more or less at nought feet. It then turned westward, out to sea, firing at parked aircraft whilst turning. One Whitley, P5024, was hit though damage was only slight and a landmark beacon was also hit. The JU88 had no desire to linger however — it disappeared into cloud as fast as it came.

Les Sidwell remembers this attack well. . ."Flying had been scrubbed and we were hanging about the crewroom that morning in hopes of a better weather forecast when the JU88 flew in from the sea. We had no warnings until the camp sirens sounded as he appeared. People scattered and defences opened up. We had a good view from our window of our tracers going at him at a low angle and his own tracers kicking up the ground. Mrs Williams was very angry about this attack as she had been attending a cow that was calving in a barn near the airfield boundary and a cannon shell had penetrated the roof. We were amazed that this aircraft had reached North Wales in such foul weather when everything here had been grounded that morning, and we wondered if he got back. . ."

"But all was not darkness and gloom — far from it. We had a lot of fun, like the affair of Lloyd George's statue in the Market Square, Caernarfon.

We caught buses back to camp, after an evening out, right near the statue and the big queue waiting for the last bus would urinate against the Great Man, Saturday night being the worst. Local indignation led to extra police vigilance and the scuffles and pursuits in the darkness provided a lot of entertainment for us. Feelings ran high but the problem was finally resolved in the simplest way imaginable, by moving the bus stop well away from the statue.

"Another local difficulty arose when pilots, at the conclusion of air-to-air firing exercises along the coast, relieved the tedium by flying low over Caernarfon before landing, and empty cartridge cases might be shovelled out of a hatch on to innocent Welsh people below. Such diversions inevitably caused more trouble with the police and deservedly earned us stern reprimands from our CO."

Leslie Sidwell successfully completed the Air Gunners' course and was awarded his flying brevet at a 'Wings' parade on 13th March with the added bonus of a commission. He was then posted to 23 OTU, Pershore.

A significant event, although nobody could have known it at the time, was the arrival on 14th May 1942 of Flight Lieutenant Graham as Llandwrog's SMO. Soon after taking up his responsibilities Graham became increasingly concerned at the number of flying accidents occurring in the mountains of Snowdonia when aircrew had died simply because proper medical assistance could not be got to them quickly enough. To overcome this problem a rescue organisation was set up by Flt. Lt. Graham, which from relatively primitive beginnings became quite sophisticated and served as a model for other similar units. It was in fact the birth of the Mountain Rescue Service within the RAF. The story is related in more detail in the chapter on accidents in Snowdonia.

On 28th May three of the Whitleys were removed from their routine training flights and sent to RAF Driffield for one week's detachment in order to take part in a thousand bomber raid on Cologne, one of the aircraft being subsequently reported missing.

Training continued at Llandwrog of course, and the figures for May 1942 reveal the level of activity:-

Pupil intake	— 86
Pupil output	— 44
Still training	— 122
Station strength (31-5-42)	— 35 Officers 577 Airmen
Army Attachment	2 Officers 3 Other Ranks
No.9 AOS detachment	— 8 Officers 136 Airmen

One of the airfield's shortcomings was highlighted in an accident during this month when an Anson experienced failure of both engines after take off, ironically on an engine test. It ended up by ditching in the sea just beyond runway 09. Fortunately the crew were soon picked up by a rescue launch from the ASR unit at nearby Fort Belan. But the problem facing all aircraft using Llandwrog was the proximity of the sea to runways 09 and 03. Should a take-off have to be abandoned or an emergency arise immediately after becoming airborne, as in the Anson's case, pilots had little choice but to ditch. To make matters worse the prevailing south westerly winds meant that most take-offs were from these runways and in a seaward direction. This fact caused a number of ditchings throughout the war.

During the summer of 1942 Llandwrog was involved in a peculiar organisational change when No.9 AGS was disbanded on 13th June and the airfield became a satellite of RAF Penrhos, where No.9 (0) AFU flew Ansons, mostly for navigator training. This seemed a most illogical decision considering Llandwrog's superiority in a number of ways over Penrhos. For instance it possessed tarmac runways; all night flying took place here and personnel strength at the satellite exceeded that of the parent airfield.

Following this change the Whitleys were withdrawn from service and were replaced during August by Blenheim Mk.IVs. Ten flew in on the 3rd, followed by another eight, arriving in pairs, on the 4th, 6th, 12th and 18th of August.

The training figures for that month show a pupil intake of sixty, and output of fifty eight, with another sixty pupils remaining under instruction.

With No.9 (0) AFU now using Llandwrog as a satellite many more Ansons, used for navigation training, were to be seen on the airfield. Accidents involving these aircraft occurred frequently, averaging about one per month. For instance, the losses for the year August 1942 to August 1943 were:-

      DJ125 — crashed into the sea, 8th August
      DJ117 — missing with all crew, 23rd August
      DJ126 — crashed at Wigtown, 22nd September
      DJ628 — missing after night flying exercise, 14th November
      DJ635 — crashed into Moel Eiliau mountain, 28th
               November
      DJ619 — crashed into the sea, 3rd January 1943
      DJ627 — crashed into the sea, 15th March

DJ618 — force landed in the sea off Holyhead, 29th March
EF926 — force landed near Clynnog
AX407 — disappeared during navigation exercise, 1st May
VY952 — crashed on the airfield, 28th August

Overall, some thirty aircraft were lost due to a combination of factors such as being caught in bad weather, flying into high ground, inadequate navigational aids and pilot error.

During early 1943 Llandwrog's incongruous position as a satellite of Penrhos came under review and a conference was held on 11th January to consider the position. The result was a common sense decision to reverse the roles of the two airfields. Exactly one month later, on 11th February, Penrhos became a satellite of Llandwrog, to where the SHQ was moved.

Training continued during the remainder of 1943 and into 1944 routinely and systematically, without disruption or further organisational change. A steady stream of courses came and went, although by the end of 1944 and early 1945 the output of aircrew began to decrease somewhat. During February, by which time it was clear that the end of hostilities could not be far distant, the question of peacetime use of the RAF's myriad airfields became increasingly important and the Air Ministry post-war airfields committee, after discussing the case of Llandwrog, decided it should be offered to the War Office as a base for an army co-operation unit which would work in conjunction with the Royal Artillery at Tŷ Croes, Anglesey. This was because Bodorgan, which had been the home of the local co-operation unit, was likely to close and revert to agriculture (which it did) once the war ended.

Extension of the main north-south runway was also being considered at this time, which might well have reduced the number of aircraft ending up on Dinas Dinlle beach or in the sea. Neither proposal came to pass however.

In May Flying Training Command issued instructions that the airfield would be closed and the flying unit disbanded on 14th June. During the remaining few weeks no productive flying took place as the unit's aircraft were disposed of to MUs. Within a few days of closure No.2 Aircrew Holding Unit had been set up and large numbers of aircrew began to arrive from Mona and Penrhos in addition to other stations within No.25 and 29 Group, to swell the ranks of those from Llandwrog itself before being sent to other units or returning to civilian life. At the end of June the airfield went on a Care and Maintenance basis pending firm decisions on its future use.

Within a few months the decision had been taken — Llandwrog was to become, from August 1946, a base for No.277 MU which was a Chemical Storage Unit. For the next ten years the airfield was used for storage and disposal of chemical weapons and explosives.

Chapter 6

"A Retreat from the Harshness of War"?
R.A.F. Penrhos & Hell's Mouth

Described by one airman as, "A typical pre-war regulars' hideaway, everything spick and span", Penrhos was the only airfield already in existence in Gwynedd when war broke out. As No.5 Armament Training Camp it had been used since 1937 to provide air gunnery and bombing practice for a variety of RAF units, mostly Flying Training Schools.

The airfield's beginnings in the mid 1930s had been the source of fierce argument however. Strong opposition by pacifist Welsh Nationalists to Air Ministry plans for a bombing school located on the Llŷn peninsula — a stronghold of Welsh culture — had culminated in the famous arson attack of September 1936, when some airfield huts and building materials had been set alight by three leading Nationalists. This was a final act of token defiance, when all attempts to prevent the development had failed and the three men had voluntarily given themselves up to the police. A controversial trial followed, as a result of which the trio were given short prison sentences.

When these events were taking place the inevitability of another war did not seem obvious but as the end of the decade approached it was clear, even to the most optimistic, that war with Germany was certain. From September 1939 it had become a reality and Britain was faced with the dark prospect of a long, hard fight against a formidable enemy. As far as the Welsh Nationalists were concerned, their arguments, based on moral grounds, against a bombing school in Llŷn became much less valid once war had been declared. The seriousness of the situation seemed to render all such debates irrelevant as the struggle for victory took precedence over everything and everybody.

At Penrhos the first change upon the outbreak of hostilities was a new title for the training unit. From 9th September it was to be known as No.9 Air Observers School. This came about because of the considerable re-organisation of training that took place within the RAF at this time. The School, equipped with a variety of obsolete aircraft, was organised into four flights — 'A' had target-towing Wallaces and Henleys, 'B' used Fairey Battles for bombing practice whilst gunnery training was the responsibility of 'C' and 'D' Flights, flying Hawker Demons and Handley Page Harrows. In December 1939 they were joined by 'C' Flight of No.1 AACU, operating Henleys, and then in February 1940 by 'J' Flight also operating Henleys for target towing. These aircraft were used primarily for artillery co-operation duties with the army on their ranges at Tonfannau.

The airfield itself was of a roughly circular pattern with its grass surface providing a maximum take-off and landing run of 860 yards. Running along the north western edge was a line of small hills about 100 feet high and 400 yards from the perimeter whilst on the southern side the surrounding land was about 20 feet or so lower than the airfield. This 'drop' was a permanent hazard for aircraft.

Thirteen hangars had been constructed, three Bellmans, nine Blisters and one 'F' type Flight Shed of pre-war design with side opening doors. All the domestic and technical sites were concentrated on the northern side of the airfield.

With the war just a few weeks old a little excitement and mystery came to the station when, on 23rd October, the duty pilot took off early in the morning and soon after witnessed what seems to have been a clandestine rendezvous between a fishing boat and a submarine in the coastal waters nearby. The station record states: "A pilot whilst flying on duty at 0745 hours saw the conning tower of a submarine two miles south of St. Tudwal's Islands, (two small offshore islands near the village of Abersoch). The submarine was submerging and proceeding in a southerly direction. A fishing boat in the vicinity may have been giving supplies to the submarine. The number of the fishing boat was given to the police superintendent at Pwllheli and HQ Coastal Command were informed of the incident by signal."

Further suspicious activity was seen and recorded on the 26th. . ."At approximately 0200 hours two white lights were observed at sea off Llanbedrog Head by the guard at the entrance to the station. The local coastguard investigated and it was discovered the ship had approached St. Tudwal's Islands and moored there. It subsequently moved to Llanbedrog Head. No details of the ship are known. The Senior Naval Officer at Liverpool was informed by telephone, and wanted further particulars. Accordingly a Battle took off at 0730 and located the ship. The pilot could not make out the name but said it was a small cargo boat at anchor. At about 9.15 it moved into Abersoch Bay and the following particulars were obtained from the coastguard — the *Eden Vale* from Wexford, flying the Irish flag. The SNO Liverpool said he would take any necessary action."

This episode resulted in a decision to keep one Battle in an armed state and at full readiness in case of further U-boat activity. Nothing more was seen however until 1st April 1940 when the local coastguard once again reported a U-boat in the vicinity. The duty Battle took off to investigate but found nothing.

On the following day one of the staff pilots on a training flight spotted a U-boat which was probably the one previously observed by coastguards. Again the Battle took off to search but failed to find the elusive submarine. No subsequent sightings were made and this proved to be the end of the affair.

At the beginning of November 1939 Penrhos had yet another change of title when it became No.9 Bombing and Gunnery School and a few weeks later suffered one of the worst accidents of this period when Battles L5255 and L5256 collided in mid-air on the 24th. One was taking off and the other landing when they collided in the circuit because of inadequate look-out by both pilots. Six men were killed in the crash.

During the early part of 1940 training continued apace with, for example, No.14 Air Observers Course completing their training on 16th March with 32 successful pupils out of 34. No.7 Air Gunners Course completed their training on the same day and achieved 100% success with no failures at all amongst the 30 pupils.

As always there were many mishaps and accidents, some with a touch of humour, such as the one caused by the trainee gunner of Battle P2259 from No.12 OTU. On 20th May during air firing exercises he managed to put a round into the radiator of his own aircraft causing failure of the cooling system. The Battle force landed, luckily with minor damage only but no doubt with a highly embarrassed gunner on board.

Another mishap which must have been a source of great amusement involved the station commander who one day decided to take a flight in a Battle. There at the time was R. Morris of Newtown, then an LAC with the ground crew of 'B' Flight. He describes what happened. . ."The CO duly took off and the ground crew stood by on the tarmac in front of the hangar as it was not anticipated that he would be very long. When he was eventually seen circling before landing it was noted that his undercarriage was not down, and as he was making his landing approach his 'cart' was still up — panic! panic! Eventually he came in and made a lovely belly flop. The fire wagon and ambulance dashed out expecting all sorts of problems, but on reaching the aircraft they found the CO complaining that 'some damn horn' was blowing behind his head!" It was of course the undercarriage warning horn and it was not the first or the last time this had happened in the RAF.

During the early summer of 1940 a number of changes were taking place at Penrhos' gunnery/bombing range — the dramatically named Hell's Mouth — a large expanse of sandy beach about eight miles away from the airfield. Three Bellman hangars to store and service a few reserve aircraft were being erected in addition to the extension of the small grass landing area. This was part of a plan to make the site a Relief Landing Ground for Penrhos and for more general use as an emergency landing ground.

Also, a moving target range was being built near the beach. This consisted of a length of track similar to a narrow gauge railway on which a small truck ran. Mounted upon this truck was a model of an aircraft at which trainee gunners fired from ground turrets as the model moved along its track.

By July the hangars and aprons were completed, the moving target range in use, but extension of the landing ground was proceeding rather more slowly. In fact the work was not completed until May 1941.

Back at Penrhos, during the summer of 1940 the main changes included replacement of Demons by Whitleys and the arrival of a group of Polish officers and NCOs to take up flying duties and assist in the training of Polish aircrew.

On 20th September the first landing by a Spitfire at Penrhos took place. The aircraft was piloted by Pilot Officer Ross Jones of 266 Squadron. He was a native of Pwllheli and had been given permission by his squadron commander to fly from Hornchurch in order to visit his seriously ill mother, living in Abererch.

When he arrived he was refused permission to land because it was feared the airfield was too small for a Spitfire to land safely. However, Ross Jones continued with his landing, which he accomplished successfully. He was then hauled in front of the station commander who proceeded to admonish him for disobeying orders but after an explanation was given, and an apology, Ross Jones was provided with the CO's personal car and driver to take him the last few miles of his journey to Abererch!

But the biggest surprise of that period had been a few weeks earlier when on 9th July a Dornier Do17 suddenly appeared over the airfield and carried out a bombing attack in addition to machine gunning parked aircraft. Two officers were killed, Flying Officer B. Page and Pilot Officer G. Goldsmith-Jones; two Henleys (L3290 and L3359) of No.1 AACU were destroyed; three blocks of officers' quarters demolished and a hangar damaged.

Following this unexpected attack the airfield was hurriedly camouflaged by painting dark lines across the ground to give the impression, from the air, of fields and hedges. All roofs and roads were toned down also.

At first it seemed this was just an isolated incident as no further raids took place for nearly three months but early in October three attacks came in quick succession. The first, at dawn on the 2nd, was again carried out by a Dornier Do17 which came in at two hundred feet and repeated the bombing and machine gunning of the first raid. Five airmen were injured, one seriously, some contractor's buildings were demolished, the Air Ministry Works Office was damaged and also motor vehicles as a result of this attack.

On the 3rd another lone aircraft flew in at dusk and dropped a stick of ten bombs just south of Tudweiliog. It was presumed the target was the radar station at Nefyn, and not Penrhos.

Then on the third successive day, another attack came at first light when three Dornier 17s swooped low over the airfield dropping bombs and incendiaries. Luckily no casualties resulted from this raid but the landing ground was cratered, the offices of OC Flying and 'A', 'B' and 'C' Flights demolished, the main hangar was damaged and so were the workshops, the gas defence store plus the fabric workshop.

A considerable amount of flying kit kept in the demolished Flight huts was destroyed or damaged in this raid but the loss was not total however. Lengths of parachute silk were salvaged and presented to girl friends to be used for making underwear or whatever — such are the fortunes of war!

Some straffing of Pwllheli and the marine craft Air Sea Rescue unit in the harbour also took place. Just outside the town a hapless farm worker found himself being machine gunned by one of these aircraft. He escaped this frightening experience unharmed but some sheep were killed.

After a few weeks of respite two further attacks came on the 9th and 10th. At 6.10 p.m. on the 9th, in conditions of poor visibility and low cloud a JU88 suddenly appeared and flew over the airfield at a height of 100 feet with guns blazing whilst dropping bombs and incendiaries.

The duty officer that evening was Flying Officer Ian Ryall, who recalls that he had just driven his car to the far side of the airfield in order to check two Lewis gun emplacements when the JU88 made its unexpected appearance. Ryall threw himself to the ground but he was not aware of any personal danger, being far more concerned about the fate of his car which seemed to him to be drawing all the fire! However, neither he or his car was hit, the only damage being some cratering. Thirty minutes later another aircraft attacked, this time causing damage to a hangar and the station commander's office. In both cases complete surprise was achieved by the raiders.

On the following day another attempt to bomb Penrhos was made when three aircraft dropped bombs from a high altitude. The first salvo fell in wet marshy ground near Llanbedrog and did not explode, the second fell at Pensarn, near Pwllheli, with no damage caused except a few craters. The third salvo was nearer the target, falling just outside the airfield perimeter. Of the ten bombs dropped five failed to explode whilst the rest merely caused cratering.

When considering these raids the first question that comes to mind is obvious — why was Penrhos singled out by the Luftwaffe? It was an ordinary training airfield in a rearward area, of no great significance, certainly no more so than any other similar airfield in the north west, yet it was attacked no less than six times. Why?

Most probably the reason lay in an overestimation by German intelligence of the airfield's importance, arising from the enormous publicity created by Welsh Nationalist opposition to Penrhos in the 1930s.

Following these raids urgent protection was necessary and so on 12th October a flight of six Spitfires from 611 Squadron, Tern Hill, arrived to provide defence cover. Three of the aircraft returned to their base on the 21st however.

Also during October the ground defence personnel were sent to the Hell's Mouth ranges in order to improve their aim by firing at a drogue towed by a Westland Wallace. In addition to these precautions the school's Battles had been hastily modified by fitting extra guns — on a Scarf ring in the observers position, for example. A few were fitted with rear facing guns under the fuselage to cover the blind spot. The method of operation was for the gunner to sit on the cross step facing forward, observing through a mirror any possible attacker. Whether such a system would work or not was never put to the test. In addition some of the Battles carried gas canisters (thought to contain mustard gas) on each wing but their existence was kept as secret as possible.

Another precaution to minimise damage in the event of attack was to disperse the aircraft around the perimeter every night. They had to be taxied by aircrew who often had to walk back to their crewrooms. This nightly chore proved to be very unpopular and any excuse would be used to avoid being involved. The Poles, for instance, who usually understood English quite well, inexplicably lost their understanding of the language when asked to assist!

However, all of these precautions were unnecessary because the Luftwaffe never attacked Penrhos again although this could not have been known at the time of course.

On 21st December the Spitfires of 611 Squadron, who had experienced nothing more stimulating than routine patrols, were replaced by a flight of

Hurricanes from 312 (Czech) Squadron, based at Speke, but they also found themselves flying endless routine patrols week after week.

This period of inactivity ended abruptly on 14th March 1941 when a JU88 was intercepted and shot down. The victorious pilot, Flight Lieutenant Dawbarn, reported as follows:-

"At 11.05 Green section was ordered to patrol Penrhos at 25,000 feet. I was Green leader and began to orbit base. At 11.18 at 14,000 feet I was ordered to vector 300° — bogey (enemy aircraft) approaching from the north west at 10,000 feet. I lost height to 11,000 feet and after 4 minutes I saw the bogey at 8,000 feet. We were up sun. I ordered Green 2 (Sergeant Stehlik) to break and position himself for quarter attack. The enemy aircraft was confirmed as a JU88.

"I opened fire at 200 yards for 2 seconds in a diving attack and hit the port engine which ceased to function. The enemy aircraft turned south and we engaged in synchronised quarter attacks. The starboard engine failed and I assume Green 2 was responsible for this. The enemy aircraft slowly lost height to 300 feet above the sea — during which time I and Green 2 attacked until our ammunition was exhausted. There was heavy return fire but it was ineffective. It hit the sea at 11.27 hours and sank immediately. A dinghy appeared but sank in 30 seconds. One crewman was seen to float for a few seconds, then sank."

Position: 25 miles south of Bardsey.

Landed at Base 11.50

signed, Flt.Lt. A. M. Dawbarn

But Flight Lieutenant Dawbarn himself was shot down and presumed drowned only a few weeks later.

During the afternoon of 10th April he and his wingman were ordered to intercept a German aircraft approaching from the Irish Sea. Contact was made about thirty miles from the coast but during the attack Dawbarn's Hurricane received hits which set the engine on fire. He reported this by radio and as nothing further was heard it was assumed that he had ditched. His wingman did not see what happened as he was continuing with his attack on the German aircraft. Then finding himself alone he broke off and began to search for Flight Lieutenant Dawbarn. Shortage of fuel forced him to return to base without locating his leader. Other aircraft and ships continued searching until nightfall but without success and so the search was abandoned. Dawbarn was never seen again.

Shortly after this loss 312's Hurricanes left Penrhos, which had not been attacked for six months, and moved to Valley where they rejoined the rest of the Squadron recently arrived from Speke.

Not wishing to leave the airfield completely unprotected, although the danger now seemed to have decreased, the RAF decided that a decoy 'Q' site would be desirable. Accordingly, Colonel Turner's department investigated possible sites and eventually one was chosen on a remote headland near Porth Ceiriad, seven miles away. It came into operation in November 1941 and remained so until November 1943 by which time its usefulness was over.

During 1941 Penrhos, now free from attack, was training aircrew as busily as ever but still with obsolete aircraft. In June this situation was improved somewhat by the start of a major re-equipping programme whereby 26 Ansons and 53 Blenheims were to replace the obsolete machines then in use, such as Wallaces, Demons and Harrows. Defiants and Lysanders also arrived to act as target towers.

This increase in establishment meant that the available accommodation was insufficient to meet the needs of all units on the station and so to relieve the pressure it was decided that 'C' Flight of No.1 AACU would move to Tywyn at the end of June. This was quite logical as the Flight co-operated mostly with the Royal Artillery camp at Tonfannau which was closer to Tywyn than Penrhos.

Before the transfer took place one of the Flight's pilots managed, albeit unintentionally, to claim an aviation record by being the first to land an aircraft on St. Tudwal's Islands.

On 19th June 1941, to quote the unit's official recored, "A Magister piloted by Flight Sergeant Ollier attempted to proceed to Farnborough but was compelled to force land on St. Tudwal's Islands owing to engine failure. The pilot and his passenger were not spotted for two hours during which time they were under bombardment from practice bombs. This was the first aircraft to land on this island and it was a good effort to have done relatively small damage to the aircraft. The aircraft finished only ten yards from the bombing target and was thus immune from any danger of being hit", (?!).

As planned, the unit departed for Tywyn on 28th June. Meanwhile the Blenheims and Ansons were assimilated into Penrhos' training routine during the remainder of 1941. Six Ansons left in January 1942 to form a permanent night flying detachment at Llandwrog.

One factor common to both airfields was the presence of an inbuilt hazard resulting from construction and siting. Whilst Llandwrog had to contend with the proximity of the sea to its runways, Penrhos had its 'drop' — a twenty foot difference in height between the airfield boundary on its southern side and the surrounding, rather marshy, land. It was essentially an airfield built for slow pre-war biplanes and the more powerful types of aircraft that came into service in wartime had to land carefully and their pilots always had to be fully aware of the lack of space.

Should an aircraft fail to take off or make use of the maximum landing space available there was always the danger of sliding over the edge — a fate which befell many. An eye witness account of two incidents gives some impression of this hazard;

> "A Catalina was coming in low from the north obviously about to land. It skimmed the hangars by a few feet and made a perfect landing using every inch of the grass field. As it came to a standstill it teetered on the edge then rolled with great dignity down a steep embankment. Its American crew climbed out safely."

This was, in fact, a US Naval Catalina which was forced to land because of engine trouble on 6th November 1942.

> "On another occasion an OTU Wellington in some sort of trouble managed to land at Penrhos but taking off presented a problem. The aircraft was wheeled to the most northerly point among the hangars and faced into wind. The tail was raised on trestles and scores of men hung on to the tailplane while the engines were run up. The men let go and away she went over the grass clearing the specially shortened telephone poles with just inches to spare."

Another instance of this problem, especially acute for 'heavies', was the forced landing in bad weather of Halifax BB215 of 405 Squadron in December 1942. After landing it could not stop within the space available, hit a parked Anson and then, to quote the station record, "slipped over the edge."

Of course, a pilot who found himself in the unenviable position of running out of landing space could attempt to swerve his aircraft, which was a natural and instinctive reaction. Many did carry out this manoeuvre but frequently the result was damage to the undercarriage and Penrhos' operations record book has many examples of this type of mishap. For instance Anson N9562, whose pilot overshot landing at night on 13th January 1942 and then swerved, causing collapse of the aircraft's port undercarriage.

But to turn to the actual training that went on at Penrhos, what was it like, as an experience, for the many young men that arrived here to become navigators and air gunners? Perhaps some first-hand accounts will provide answers to this question. The story of Geoffrey Hall, for example, who began training as a navigator in 1942. . ."After a few weeks elementary maths, morse and navigation instruction at Brighton, Torquay and Eastbourne I was posted to Penrhos. The aircraft were Ansons and from here we made many navigational exercise flights over the Irish Sea using the Isle of Man and southern Scotland as turning points.

"As recruits we had expected to find keen, immaculately dressed officers offering precise guidance in navigational techniques. Instead we were disappointed to be led one morning to a rather worn looking Anson by a tousle-headed lad in a boiler suit and told to hop in while he climbed into the pilot's seat. They were fine, experienced fliers though hard and cynical from their operational tours. Quite rightly they did not trust our calculations and when our ETAs ran out and we insisted we were over the airfield they took one glance at the cloud layer below and flew due west for a long time to make sure they were well over the sea before descending.

"Sometimes these men needed to let off steam and I remember a hair raising unscheduled low-level over Rhyl where I was told to check the time by the Town Hall clock. Even worse was a deliberate spin over Caernarfon. I shall never forget the castle slowly revolving below and thinking that my last resting place would be within its walls.

"During our navigational trips we occasionally flew over Snowdonia and we noticed a fair amount of wreckage near the mountain summits. Once we saw what we thought was new wreckage in the Carneddau and noted the map reference but a subsequent air search by experienced men revealed nothing.

"While at Penrhos I drew the attention of the Watch Office to a Spitfire which swept down over the marshes from the sea but then apparently disappeared. I never knew the fate of the pilot or his machine but next day there was a row of bent machine guns lying in the grass outside the guardroom with other small pieces of wreckage."

This was probably a Spitfire from 41 Squadron which crash landed on marshy ground just off the airfield edge on 26th October 1942.

"For night flying we were posted temporarily to Llandwrog near Caernarfon, an airfield equipped with runways, built on the edge of the sea. Here we were told that it was the navigator's job to wind the undercarriage up and down by hand and on no account were we to confuse the undercarriage wheel with the flap wheel on the other side of the seat. Several Ansons lay in the sea just off the coast due to this error, so we were told. We lost one or two Ansons at night due, I believe, to severe icing in 'shower clouds'. Training was accelerated due, no doubt, to the forthcoming Battle of the Ruhr and we often carried three trainee navigators at night. One did all the work, calculating courses and keeping a strict log: another took a few star shots with a sextant when he felt like it and the third usually went to sleep on a heap of parachutes at the rear. Asleep or not, his flying hours counted along with the more active trainees.

"We returned to Penrhos feeling like veterans and finished the course with some cross-countries usually making a circuit of the West Midlands. The Shropshire Plain was an area across which routes were chosen, Ironbridge being a favourite turning point.

"The highlight of the course was to have been a low level cross-country, flying down one of the east-west Welsh valleys and returning over the Shropshire plain and the Vale of Clwyd. We were briefed for this event but it was suddenly cancelled; we had a few days leave and were then posted to OTUs." Geoffrey Hall eventually became a navigator in Bomber Command.

Another personal account comes from Squadron Leader G. Gray, DFC, AFC, who underwent training as an Air Gunner. He embarked upon his flying career with six weeks of ITW training, following completion of which he was re-classified from AC2 to LAC — a move which was fully approved as it meant an increase in pay from 2/- (10 pence) per day to 3/6d (17 pence). George Gray was at Penrhos from 6th January until 8th March 1941. . ."I arrived by train at Pwllheli from AONS at Prestwick via Crewe, Caernarfon and Afonwen. A local bus dropped me off at the gates of RAF Penrhos with all my kit. I was alone in the rain and sleet, the other members of the Course had not yet arrived. The corporal in the Orderly Room told me that we would be billeted in Llanbedrog.

"I stayed with a very friendly family named Hughes. It was my first visit to Wales and I was taken aback somewhat when I asked to be directed to Mrs Hughes' house to find that there were a host of families named Hughes in the village. They were a wonderful family and I'm sure that my healthy appetite did not leave them with much to spare from the Air Force's meagre allowance.

"We used to leave our billets every morning to arrive at the airfield for 8.00 a.m. parade. The bull was brief and minimal.

"Our ground instruction consisted mostly of lectures on the Browning .303 machine gun and the old Vickers G.O., the Fraser-Nash and Boulton Paul turrets and various antiquated bombs and fuses. All this theory was put into practice flying in Battles and Whitleys.

"The Fairey Battles, battered wrecks from the Battle of France, but still serviceable (glycol leaks were a menace to the poor novice bomb aimers) were used for our practice bombing. The range was just offshore at Hell's Mouth. I still remember lying prone in the rear of the Battle peering down through a large square hole in the fuselage, almost overwhelmed by the fumes of hot oil and glycol from the leaky radiator just ahead, as I tried to direct the pilot on to a small yellow triangle 6-8,000 feet below using a Mk.IX bombsight that was lowered on a strut into the slipstream.

"We used 12 lb. practice bombs only, so there was no satisfying 'crump' when they burst, just a little puff of white smoke. I had a hangup once and was horrified to watch the blasted thing hurtle towards the range control and burst on the shore.

"Our practice gunnery was carried out from Mk.II Whitleys, i.e. they had Armstrong-Siddeley Tiger radial engines, not the later Merlins. We were taken up, six pupils at a time, and we crouched in the draughty fuselage as we waited our turn to climb into the Fraser-Nash rear turret and to 'have a go'. We had to make up our own belts of ammunition and if we had a stoppage we lost marks. Wartime economy allowed us to blast away with one gun only although the turret was equipped for four guns.

"Our pilots were either very bored survivors from France or newly arrived Polish airmen, whose command of English sometimes left something to be desired, but their flying competence, however, was excellent. So you can well imagine that there were often intercom problems, given the poor quality of the carbon microphones and the TR.9 of those days.

"During the final examination I had rather an unusual experience. We were divided into squads of six for our lectures and our squad had a young Corporal Armourer as our gunnery instructor. He was a pre-war apprentice, regular, and an expert, in fact they all were. He required us among other things to strip and re-assemble the Browning .303 Machine Gun down to the last pin, and we were timed with a stop watch — the job had to be accomplished in less than two minutes. When it came to the examination at the end of the course I boasted that I would beat them all! Imagine my consternation when my turn came to go into the exam room (we did this part of the exam individually) when the corporal made me do the whole procedure blindfold.

"Everything went well until I came to put the breech block back in and pull the cocking handle back. The blasted thing refused to operate and in my embarrassment I could not feel what was wrong. Matters were not improved by Corp. keeping up a running commentary of facetious remarks. Finally, in anger and frustration I ripped off the blindfold to find that Corp., laughing his head off, had dropped a matchstick into the works! My pride was properly humbled but I still came top of the Course.

"We left Penrhos on March 8th 1941 to display with some pride to our families and friends our new flying brevets (commonly known within Air Force circles as the Flying Arsehole) and newly sewn on Sergeant's stripes."

Sergeant Gray eventually joined 502 Squadron, Coastal Command in operations against U-boats in the north Atlantic and Bay of Biscay, and, as he said, "I did have more luck than most and emerged unscathed." Of the thirty others with him at Penrhos only a few survived the war. He was one of the crew of Whitley Z9190 of 502 Squadron which on 30th November 1941 made Coastal Command's first ASV kill by sinking U-206 in the Bay of Biscay. Subsequently Sergeant Gray was commissioned and pursued a successful career in the RAF, ending up with the rank of Squadron Leader. He was also awarded the DFC and AFC.

His summing up of Penrhos as, "A pleasant retreat from the harshness of war" was a sentiment echoed by others stationed there. One such person was Jim Piggott of Oldham who provides this humorous and graphic view of life for an ordinary airman.

Having failed the aircrew medical on eyesight grounds he was posted to Penrhos during the first week of January 1943 as a general duties airman. One of his first contacts was with a fearsome SWO. . ."We had to report to him to be entered on the Station Defence Staff. He looked at us and muttered, 'Wait a minute while I find my odd little book for odd little sods like you!'

"He would have a walk around the station each morning and afternoon and at his approach you could see people rushing to hide behind huts and in toilets, even the Group Captain was known to bow to the wishes of this particular one.

"As a general duties man you were fair game for almost any jobs that wanted to be done, and we were likely to be called upon for all sorts of things, such as coal collection from Pwllheli, fire pickets and attending funeral parades. The latter duty could be unpleasant as at all training stations there were large numbers of casualties resulting from flying accidents. Some of these were from Canada, New Zealand, Australia etc. and were buried locally in Pwllheli cemetery. We were always collared for these and must have done about ten. Burial took place with full military honours: brass band playing 'The Dead March' from *Saul*, arms reversed at the cemetery gates, heads lowered, with the instruction "and you looks down with a sad an 'umble expression." The worst ones were those where relatives turned up, and these could be very upsetting.

"Another of our duties was to contribute to War Weapons Weeks by marching behind brass bands around such places as Cricieth and Pwllheli in the hope of raising £5,000 to buy a Spitfire. We had a station bus to take us to these places, and those who had to attend these parades were always given a bar of chocolate by the NAAFI!

"General duties airmen were also involved in the target towing role. Drogues would be towed by Lysanders for the air gunners to shoot at, and an operator was required, his job being to let out the drogue at the beginning of practice and then drop it on the airfield afterwards. Drogue operators were paid an extra 6d (2½ pence) per day. The drogues were let out on a steel wire and an operator could easily be recognised by wearing a working uniform that was shredded through contact with snags in the wire."

Drogues that had been shot away or prematurely released carried a reward of 5/- (25 pence) for anyone that returned them to the airfield. One local man, recalling a boyhood spent near Penrhos, remembers that any drogue towing aircraft would be watched with keen interest and if a drogue happened to fall there would be a rush for the place where it fell. "It was a big thing for us children", he writes, "to go up to the aerodrome, past the main gate, and put our names in large books when we received the money."

Jim Piggott also saw some interesting visiting aircraft. . ."Early in 1943 a large aircraft came in one day and everyone, from all sections, went to see this giant in metal. Much headshaking went on as to whether it would manage to get airborne again from the grass airfield. It was a Dakota.

"One of the most interesting I ever saw was a fragile looking autogiro which came to calibrate two radar stations in the vicinity, [Nefyn and Aberdaron]. It was an Avro Rota, made under licence from the Spanish designer, Cierva."

On 14th April 1943 two Swordfishes unexpectedly turned up, their arrival being recorded thus: "At 22.15 hours two Swordfish aircraft were seen circling requesting permission to land. Attempts were made to direct the aircraft to Llandwrog but they seemed determined to land at Penrhos. As much light as possible was displayed on the airfield and both made perfect landings at 22.45."

Not every emergency ended like this however. A few weeks later, on Sunday 2nd May a Wellington in difficulties tried to land but crashed in flames just outside the airfield, killing four of the crew and injuring two others. Jim Piggott was a witness. . ."It was a day I shall never forget. We were coming back from a Sunday hike and had just booked into the guardroom. Walking on the road leading to our hut we could see on approach to the field a Wellington bomber with its starboard engine out and prop feathered. It touched down on the field and at the last minute the pilot must have decided he did not have enough room to land. He took off again, failed to gain height and must have seen there was a small hill facing him, (where the WAAF quarters were sited), banked right to avoid this obstacle, stalled and crashed in a field just in front of the camp. It being Sunday there was no fire tender crew on duty, not that it mattered anyway. I cannot think of a more fearsome sight than a crashing aircraft. . ."

"As for leisure activities at Penrhos, lack of money was the big problem, buying a packet of cigarettes, a cup of tea and a wad would just about be manageable. Many of the airmen would make models etc., and the instrument mechanics, watchmakers to a man, plied a trade cleaning watches at 4/- (20 pence) a time — more than a day's pay for two hours work!

We also had a radio, but there was only one available for the airmen's huts and this was allocated on the basis of the best turned out hut on weekly inspection. I think it was Hut No.5 that used to win it every week. The rumour was that they spent all week cleaning the bloody thing, so they hadn't much time to listen to the radio anyway! There were two shows a week at the cinema, "Charlie Chan meets Jack the Ripper" type of thing, entrance about 3d I think. Dances were also held in Pwllheli.

"Being very fond of walking most of our lot used to go out on a Sunday, (a day off for all the Station in accordance with local custom, ignoring the war) and the cookhouse used to provide us with a packed lunch. Within a couple of hours we would be exploring the local countryside and nearby hills.

"During May three of us were notified that we were posted to commence training at the Navigation School, Bridgnorth. After packing our kit, obtaining clearance from all sections, came the final, dreaded call on the SWO to be removed from the odds and sods book. I can see his pitying look now as he crossed us off various duties and his final words often come to mind — "Now you lot have had a fucking good holiday whilst you have been here, and I don't want you to ever forget it. Now piss off!"

Jim Piggott concludes, "Afterwards I served in India, Burma, Singapore, Sumatra, Java and on reflection I think he was probably right."

Another personal recollection worth recording, for the insight into life at Hell's Mouth that it provides is that of Ted Lane. Now living in Orpington, he was then one of a small group of airmen responsible for manning the bombing range at this now forgotten airfield. . ."I arrived at Penrhos from Blackpool one dark wet night in November 1942. The following day I reported to HQ and was told to pack my kit as I was being sent to a satellite station. After a lorry ride of about ten miles I arrived at a small cluster of huts that seemed to be perched on the edge of the world. It rained, the wind blew and the sea roared. This was not my idea of RAF service and I was depressed. I was to remain at Hell's Mouth until September 1943, but my depression soon went and I now look back on those months in North Wales with nostalgia and many happy memories.

"At Hell's Mouth we had the following personnel — one Officer, one Flight Sergeant, two or three Sergeants, a few Corporals, about thirty Airmen and a small group of RAF Regiment types who left sometime in February 1943.

"Our function was to operate the bombing range for aircraft at Penrhos. Out in the bay were anchored two rafts to act as targets for the trainee bomb aimers. They would fly over on a bombing run, mostly in Ansons, aim and drop twelve pound smoke bombs which would ignite on striking the sea. Positioned at points along the bay known as Quadrants we would focus telescopes on the smoke and note the compass bearing on a fixed metal ring. When the aircraft had finished bombing they would fly across the quadrants, waggle their wings, and we would then telephone our compass readings through to Penrhos. There, they would mark a 'plot' and ascertain how good the pupil bomb aimer was at his job.

"Three quadrants were used — No.1 in the south west corner of the bay, No.2 in the middle and within walking distance of the camp, No.3 in the far north west corner and the two men who manned it had to cycle there. We took turns at manning each quadrant and would be out all day, taking rations with us and cooking on a primus stove.

"At No.3 Quadrant it was always possible to buy some eggs from a nearby farm — eggs were a great luxury in those days. The memory of a sunny day waiting for the next Anson to arrive, the freshly brewed tea and your mate frying eggs, bacon and newly picked mushrooms is still fresh in the mind even now, forty years later.

"They were happy days and it was difficult to realise that a war was on. In fact when I went home on leave and saw the bomb damage in my own town outside London I felt rather guilty when I returned to the rural peace of Hell's Mouth.

"One morning an airman arrived at No.2 Quadrant and telephoned in to report that the beach was full of oranges! We all trooped down and sure enough, thousands of them everywhere, but none were edible as the salt water had got into them. We also had the odd mine washed ashore, one of which exploded, shaking the huts and breaking a few windows. Twice we had a body, one a sailor and the other an airman, both unidentifiable. On one of my many walks along the beach I found the remnants of life rafts, life boats and oil-stained life jackets that reminded me that there was a war going on out there beyond the horizon.

"One day we had an emergency landing by a Wellington. It touched down safely and the crew were given a meal in the dining hall. That afternoon the pilot decided to fly solo due to the danger of taking off from such a small field. He managed to get the aircraft airborne just as he was running out of space. Turning over the bay he waggled his wings and made off. The rest of the crew departed by road.

"We also had our own aircraft, four Blenheims and an old Whitley, none of which ever flew! Lord knows why they were there. Each morning they would be checked over and sometimes the engines would be started. They were housed in hangars in the south west corner of the camp. One day a pilot arrived from somewhere and flew the Whitley off. As he turned away, a chunk of wing fabric was seen to come adrift but he continued as if nothing had happened!

"It all came to an end for me in September 1943 when I departed to start my gunnery training course."

During its existence Hell's Mouth proved to be a safe haven for a few lost aircraft such as two Whirlwinds of 263 Squadron for instance. On 22nd May 1942 they were chasing a German bomber out over the Irish Sea when they lost radio contact with base and as their fuel was getting low the leader decided to abandon the pursuit and head for land. Eventually they made a most fortuitous landfall at Hell's Mouth and landed with their fuel tanks practically empty. Another aircraft to use the landing ground in an emergency was a P-38 Lightning from Atcham, which landed safely on 25th September 1944.

Returning to events at Penrhos, the station was visited by the Duke of Kent on 11th May 1942 as part of his tour of military establishments in North Wales. After lunch and an inspection of the airfield he departed for the Royal Navy shore establishment HMS Glendower a few miles away on the other side of Pwllheli. Glendower was in fact one of Butlin's holiday camps, requisitioned before it opened.

Apparently the journey proved a little difficult, according to *The Chronicle*, which reported:- "Wearing RAF uniform the Duke drove his own car and was held up for a short time while in a traffic block in one of the narrow streets of a North Wales market town [i.e. Pwllheli — wartime censorship prevented the newspaper from making a direct reference]. Later he lost his way on the crossroads at the other end of town and had to make enquiries from a townsman who directed him on the right road. The Duke, driving back through the town, again had to make enquiries and this time he was recognised by several people who gave him a cheer."

Administrative changes at Penrhos during 1942 began with a change of title for the training unit — from 28th February it would be known as No.9 (O) AFU.

In June Llandwrog was acquired as a satellite when No.9 AGS was disbanded and administration of the two airfields carried out from Penrhos.

Training continued without further disruption or organisational change throughout the remainder of the war, with a steady output of Air Gunners and Navigators being sent to OTUs.

During May 1945 the expected and fateful communication from Flying Training Command was received, stating that the airfield would close and go on a C. & M. basis from 14th June. On that day the remaining trainees were posted to other stations. After the cessation of flying the station's accommodation was used by No.21 ACHU until its disbandment in March 1946.

Some discussion then arose over the airfield's future, the local council, for example, thought it would be ideal for use as an educational centre but eventually in 1947 most of the domestic site was turned into a permanent home for Polish servicemen who wished to stay in Britain rather than return to their own country. The Home remains to this day — a tiny concentration of Polish culture set in the midst of this most Welsh area. Religion, in the form of the Catholic faith, plays an important part in the lives of Poles and it is rather odd when visiting Penrhos to see the icons and madonnas of that faith set amongst a well preserved group of RAF wartime utility buildings.

As far as Hell's Mouth was concerned, the RAF at first decided to continue using the ranges for gunnery and bombing practice after the war, and indeed were considering an expansion of the offshore range to take in an area eight miles seawards. This plan caused much local protest, to which the RAF bowed, although they refused to release any land. Caernarfonshire's M.P., Goronwy Roberts pressed continually for release until his persistence paid off early in 1947. By April range clearance work had begun, in order to render the land safe for agricultural use.

A visitor to this largely forgotten airfield would find little evidence today of its former existence. Nothing remains except the ruins of a few air-raid shelters and part of the perimeter track which is now a public road. The rural calm remains however, as does the great stretch of sand of Hell's Mouth.

At Penrhos the landing ground lay unused for many years, until eventually a substantial part was turned into a caravan park. A small, private landing strip was constructed on what remained, and is now used by light aircraft, particularly during the summer months.

In September 1986, fifty years after the famous arson attack, a commemorative rally was held here by the Welsh Nationalists during which an expensive and elaborate memorial plaque was unveiled. Thus the Nationalists had the last word, after all, at Penrhos.

Chapter 7

Between Mountain and Sea
R.A.F. Llanbedr

This airfield was constructed in 1940-41 on a small coastal strip known as Morfa Dyffryn near the village of Llanbedr, from which it gained its name. Intended as a forward base for daytime operations against enemy aircraft in the Irish Sea it came under the control of Valley as part of No.9 Group. There were two runways, one NE-SW 3,900 feet long and the other NW-SE with a length of 3,300 feet. Five hangars were built, one Bellman and four Blisters.

The opening up party which arrived on 23rd July 1941 found an airfield set amidst some of the grandest Welsh scenery, the sea on one side, the Rhinog mountains on the other, Harlech castle atop its crag to the north, the beautiful Mawddach estuary to the south and Cader Idris mountain beyond.

However, they had more urgent things to do than admire the view. The airfield had to be prepared for a fighter squadron, as yet unspecified. But in the event Llanbedr's first occupier turned out to be a rather less warlike detachment of six Ansons from No.6 Air Observer and Navigation School, which arrived on 24th August from Staverton. On 20th September one aircraft with five men on board returning to Llanbedr from Worthy Down was lost when it crashed in the sea near Bardsey Island, disappearing without a trace of wreckage. The pilot's body was eventually recovered from the sea near RAF Bodorgan a month later.

On 4th October the expected fighters arrived at last — Spitfires of 74 Squadron from RAF Acklington, in Northumberland. In command was Squadron Leader P. Ridley, DFC. One aircraft crashed on landing but the pilot was unhurt, and a few days later Squadron Leader Ridley himself decided to bale out of his Spitfire when the undercarriage failed to lower. He made a safe landing but his aircraft crashed into the sea.

Once settled in, the squadron proceeded to carry out convoy patrols and soon an opportunity for combat arose, when, on the 13th, aircraft were scrambled to intercept enemy raiders over St. George's Channel but no contact was made. Again, on 8th November four Spitfires were airborne at 7.30 a.m. to intercept an enemy bomber which had dropped bombs on Holyhead. Later, all available aircraft were airborne but luck was not with them and none succeeded in intercepting the raider.

On 27th November two of 74 Squadron's pilots, Pilot Officer Williams and Sergeant Ingle were ordered to intercept three JU88s off St. David's Head. After making contact with the enemy aircraft Pilot Officer Williams attacked one from astern and caused enough damage to justify a claim of "probable". He then gave chase to the other two aircraft but his Spitfire was hit by return fire from the JU88s and dived into the sea. Williams' body was washed up on the beach at Pembroke on 17th December.

The squadron lost another pilot a few days later when Sergeant Brown, a Canadian, crashed in the sea. Sadly, another sergeant pilot was killed on the day before Christmas after an accident whilst carrying out some formation flying. On a brighter, more seasonal note some of the airmen went out carol singing in the locality of Llanbedr.

On 13th January 1942 74 Squadron was ordered to move to Long Kesh, Northern Ireland, forthwith. Two days later 5 Officers and 130 Airmen left by rail whilst two Harrow transports landed to take the rest of the squadron by air to their new station. On the 21st, with everyone ready to move, two sections were scrambled to intercept an enemy aircraft reported over Anglesey but no contact was made. The squadron finally departed on the 24th when thirteen Spitfires and the two Harrows took off for Long Kesh though no doubt the Spitfires arrived long before the Harrows.

The next squadron at Llanbedr was No.131, commanded by Squadron Leader Pedley, who arrived from Atcham on 8th February, a month during which Drem lighting was installed at the airfield. A few weeks later 131 transferred to Valley, on 3rd March. At the end of the month Llanbedr's first station commander, Squadron Leader Prior was replaced by Squadron Leader E. Bullimore.

Meanwhile, at Valley the sand problem, which had not yet been cured, was causing a great deal of trouble for the squadron and making it almost impossible to keep their Spitfires serviceable. In addition problems arose over the quality of R/T communication between Valley and Llanbedr because of the intervening high ground. As a result 131 was forced to return to Llanbedr sooner than planned, arriving back in mid April. In May, after carrying out some joint exercises with the army, they were on the move again, this time to Merston. On 4th May 232 Squadron was posted to Llanbedr from Atcham and remained until August. The squadron divided its time between routine Irish Sea patrols and working up to full operational capacity. Late in June the squadron went on temporary detachment to RAF Merston in order to take part in the raid on Dieppe. This raid had been planned since April and was due to be put into operation on 4th July but unfavourable weather caused a postponement until the 8th. However, the poor weather continued and so the raid was abandoned and 232 Squadron returned to Llanbedr on the same day. All the squadron's Spitfires returned safely except one which crash landed at Penrhos with propeller trouble. Early in August 232 departed for Turnhouse, near Edinburgh.

Following 232s move to Scotland the next fighter squadron at Llanbedr was 41, which arrived on 9th August 1942 equipped with Spitfire Vs, and led by Squadron Leader G. C. Hyde. They were lucky enough to experience combat on the 14th when, just before mid-day, Yellow Section was ordered to intercept a JU88 east of Dublin. The interception was successful and hits were observed but the raider managed to escape towards Eire.

In the meantime a decision had been taken to carry out the combined operations raid on Dieppe, postponed in July. The new date was to be 19th August and 41 squadron was amongst those scheduled to take part. Accordingly the squadron left Llanbedr on the 16th for RAF Tangmere. Whilst en-route one of the pilots crashed near Henley-on-Thames and was killed.

This time the raid did take place as planned and turned out to be a disaster with very high numbers of casualties and nothing in the form of any tangible gains. Along with other units 41 Squadron took its share of the losses, six pilots being reported missing including the CO.

Subsequently there was so little action at Llanbedr that the squadron almost became non-operational and morale tended to suffer as a consequence.

On 22nd October the squadron experienced a further blow to morale when three Spitfires of 'A' Flight and their pilots were lost in an accident whilst practising formation flying in cloud. Six miles east of Tywyn they flew, in formation, into Hendre mountain, killing the unfortunate pilots instantly. A shepherd found the wreckage two days later.

During the late summer of 1942 Llanbedr was used by American units as well as the RAF. Lightnings from USAAF fighter squadrons based at Atcham were sent on short detachments for operational training including air to air firing practice. The first to arrive were eight Lightnings of the 48th Fighter Squadron late in August, followed by sixteen aircraft from the 49th in mid September. Two of these aircraft were ordered to intercept a German aircraft near Carnsore Point, Eire, on 26th September but failed to make contact whilst another Lightning was lost when it crashed in the sea off Harlech on the 27th.

A target towing service was provided for the fighter squadrons by Lysanders of the USAAFs No.2025 Gunnery Flight at Llanbedr. In addition an air-to-ground firing range was located on Tal-y-Bont beach, plus a number of similar ranges at Trawsfynydd, and a buoy off the coast was also used for bombing practice.

At the same time a small Naval detachment from 776 Squadron, RNAS Speke was established at Llanbedr, with a couple of target towing Skuas. This detachment remained for nearly two years before moving to Mona in April 1944.

During the last two months of 1942 Llanbedr's resident fighter squadron, No.41, had little but routine flying to carry out, interspersed with a few scrambles but no contact was made as a result. The flying hours accumulated during December, for instance, were 51 hours operational, 289 hours daytime non-operational, 22 hours night flying and 2 hours of convoy duty.

This pattern of activity continued into 1943, with some army exercises and fruitless scrambles to relieve the routine of endless patrols. The squadron had a fatal accident early in February when one of the sergeant pilots crashed during a 'beat-up' of Pwllheli. Later in the month it was announced that the squadron was to move to High Ercall on the 25th. When the day of the move came 41's CO wrote: "A hearty farewell to Llanbedr, where the squadron has been recuperating. . .", and then, during the final departure he 'killed' his engine whilst trying to take-off, much to the amusement of station personnel!

After 41 Squadron had gone the airfield lost its operational status as a fighter base and no other squadrons were allocated for defensive purposes. From this point onwards until the war ended Llanbedr was used primarily for armament practice.

The next unit to arrive was 1486 Gunnery Flight which came from Valley at the beginning of July 1943 in order to create space at that airfield for the 'Transat' scheme to be put into operation. Other aircraft using Llanbedr during July included two Beaufighters from 406 Squadron, Valley, on air firing exercises, a de Havilland Dominie (the military version of the Rapide) from Sealand, which gave local ATC cadets air experience flights, a Botha which force-landed with engine trouble, an Oxford, an ATA Anson, a Spitfire of 322 Squadron which had a taxying accident resulting in considerable damage to the aircraft, and four Mosquitoes engaged on air-to-air firing exercises.

In mid October 1486 Flight disbanded and reformed as No.12 Armament Practice Camp. This unit had two Miles Masters, two Martinets and three Lysanders. Six Martinets had been delivered but were without radios and so could not be flown until the necessary equipment had been fitted. During November another armament practice camp, no.13, formed here with similar aircraft.

Earlier in the month, on the 3rd, a Wellington had experienced severe icing conditions at 15,000 feet over the nearby mountains but luckily managed to land at Llanbedr. On the following day its luck ran out, when, a few moments after take-off it crashed half a mile from the airfield, killing one of the crew and seriously injuring two others.

The station strength at this time was 22 Officers and 142 other ranks.

From November 1943 until May 1944 a succession of twenty six fighter squadrons, British and Allied, came to Llanbedr on short detachments of ten days or so in order to carry out armament practice. The aircraft flown by these squadrons were Spitfires, Mustangs and Typhoons. Air-to-ground ranges at Dyffryn were used in addition to drogues towed by Martinets.

All of this was in preparation for the Allied invasion of France, which came about with the Normandy landings of June 1944.

The first squadron to arrive for training was 322 (Dutch) Squadron in mid November 1943 followed by 310 (Czech) Squadron at the beginning of December. Others were, for example, 312 (Czech), 331 (Norwegian), 485 (New Zealand) and 340 (Free French) Squadrons. To illustrate the intensity of flying, sorties flown on 5th, 6th and 7th December were 150, 151 and 148 respectively.

The vast majority of these sorties were incident free but during March 1944 two fatal accidents occurred on the Dyffryn range when one of the range control airmen was, sadly, shot during firing exercises and secondly, a Spitfire of 602 Squadron crashed, killing the pilot. Nearly two thousand sorties were flown during the month. In April range facilities were extended with the opening of a bombing range at Penychain.

May 1944 saw the placing of navigation obstruction lights on the surrounding mountains in order to try and cut down the number of accidents, and it was also a month when the station commander had a nasty experience after the engine of his Magister failed on take-off, the aircraft subsequently crashing in the sea. Luckily he and his passenger were unhurt but the Magister was a total loss.

During June Llanbedr's armament practice units were disbanded, their work more or less finished, although the Americans continued to use the ranges. In mid July a group of ATA pilots flew in to collect eight Martinets for final disposal and within a week every aircraft had gone, with the exception of the station commander's Magister. Many of the station's personnel were also transferred to other units as Llanbedr wound down, its wartime role to all intents and purposes at an end.

At the beginning of September a Fortress from RAF Atcham landed, but overshot, causing slight damage and on the 13th a Wellington also overshot and crashed, fortunately without causing any injury to the crew.

During October 1944 Martinets from Tywyn used the airfield because their own grass field had been rendered unserviceable by heavy rain. Thereafter Llanbedr was used for emergency landings and bad weather diversions only, with little of note taking place.

When the war ended the airfield remained open and indeed in May 1945 631 Squadron moved from Tywyn, with target-towing Vengeances. On 15th September, in common with many other RAF stations, Llanbedr played host to the public during an Open Day to commemorate the Battle of Britain victory. Large crowds turned up for this event and one hundred cars were counted, which by today's standards seems insignificant but in the immediate post-war period must have been quite a number.

When the time came to consider the airfield's long term future the Air Ministry had four options:- a) transfer to the War Office, b) development for civil aviation purposes, c) use as a substitute for Penrhos, d) use as a bad weather diversion airfield, but in the event none of these possible options came about. Llanbedr was eventually to become an outstation of RAE Farnborough, thus entering upon a new and interesting lease of life as a centre for the operation and development of pilotless target drones — a role which it carries out to this day.

Chapter 8

A Forgotten Airfield
R.A.F. Tywyn

This small grass airfield located near the village of Tywyn, ten miles south of Barmouth, was established in the summer of 1940 as a base for an army co-operation unit working mostly in conjunction with the Royal Artillery gunnery range at Tonfannau. It came under the control of No.70 Group, Army Co-operation Command, itself newly formed that summer. The airfield was constructed on land belonging to Morfa Farm.

The process of opening up the new station seems to have been a rather casual affair spread over many months with the HQ building, for example, being taken over on 19th October. In November the opening up officer, Flight Lieutenant Irens, was promoted to Squadron Leader and appointed CO of Tywyn. Under his command he had two flights of No.1 AACU — 'U' Flight, who moved from St. Athan during the autumn, with Queen Bee pilotless drones, and 'C' Flight which came from Penrhos in June 1941, equipped with Hawker Henleys. The unit's aircraft were housed in two Bellman hangars, two Blisters and two Bessoneaux. Station strength was to be quite modest — 12 Officers and 226 Airmen.

Before target towing operations could begin however, it seemed that invasion was imminent when on 8th September 1940 a Magister from Penrhos landed with the dramatic message that invasion by German forces was about to take place. Secret papers were prepared for burning and the number of armed guards around the airfield doubled, but it was, of course, a false alarm.

Like Llandwrog and Llanbedr, Tywyn was situated on the coast but unlike the others it had a grass surface which was prone to flooding. This fault was brought to light early in the airfield's history when Bristol Beaufort L4462 made an emergency landing in November 1940 after experiencing engine trouble on a flight from St. Eval to Abbotsinch. On the following day the airfield had to be declared unserviceable because of heavy rain, which effectively imprisoned the Beaufort for another two days before the condition of the airfield improved sufficiently for the aircraft to depart. On the same day a Magister was collected from Penrhos as a station hack. Flooding was particularly bad during the winter months and on a number of occasions the airfield became so waterlogged that the unit's aircraft had to move temporarily to Llanbedr.

Meanwhile, the station commander had been to Aberporth to discuss the details of a transmitter to be installed at Tywyn so that Queen Bee operations could begin. The necessary transmitter arrived in November but it took another three months of delay, sorting out teething troubles, before the first radio controlled flight took place on 25th February 1941. Early in March the first Queen Bee take off under radio control, with a safety pilot on board, was successfully achieved and so with this final hurdle overcome, the nearby Army artillery unit was duly advised that Tywyn was now ready to commence its co-operation role.

The Queen Bee was relatively sophisticated for its time and was successful as a target drone but tended to suffer damage to its control system from near misses by artillery fire. Losses occurred fairly frequently and regularly throughout the period of operation at Tywyn, averaging about one or two aircraft every month.

The Henleys flown by 'C' Flight were not free of problems either. The type was not specifically designed for target-towing and the heavy loads of drogue towing imposed considerable strain on engines. Malfunction and failure were frequent occurrences resulting in many accidents, some of which were fatal. Henley L3284, for instance, force landed half a mile from the airfield in June 1941 killing both pilot and drogue operator, and also L3435, which crashed offshore near Tonfannau after engine failure in May 1942. The drogue operator was thrown clear but unfortunately the pilot, a 24 year old New Zealander, was drowned after being knocked unconscious by the impact.

On 1st June 1941 a Junkers JU88 crashed in the sea off Barmouth whilst returning to its base in France and some time after, the bodies of two crewmen were washed up near Tywyn, Ober-Leutnant Theo Sandgathe on 26th June and Unter-Officer Willi Freitag in July. They were buried locally but later their remains were reburied at the German military cemetery, Cannock.

During February 1942 the Queen Bees and Henleys were augmented by the arrival of two Lysanders on detachment from No.6 AACU to provide extra army co-operation duty. Towards the end of the year some reorganisation took place when 'C' Flight became No.1605 AAC Flight in November and on the 23rd took delivery of three Martinets. But at the same time one of the unit's Henleys was lost when L3324 was flown into cloud obscured high ground near Penygroes, Caernarfon. The pilot was killed instantly.

The Martinets were an improvement as they were designed for target-towing — the first aircraft type in fact to enter service with the RAF purely to perform this kind of work. Based on the Miles Master but with a longer nose and particular attention paid to the cooling of the Bristol

Mercury engine due to the heavy demands of towing, Martinets proved far more reliable than the Henleys.

The tedious routine of target towing was relieved on 16th December by the unexpected arrival of 12 P-38 Lockheed Lightnings of the USAAF's 97th Fighter Squadron. Whilst en-route from Northern Ireland to St. Eval bad weather caused a diversion to Tywyn which itself was waterlogged. One lightning overshot into a gun pit on the airfield boundary resulting in Cat.E damage — i.e. a 'write off'. The remaining fighters departed for St. Eval two days later, their final destination being North Africa.

During their brief stay the American pilots made the most of the situation by getting to know some of the local girls at a dance. Apparently it became something of a wild affair, especially when one over-enthusiastic pilot drew a revolver and began to fire shots through the roof! This caused havoc and Military Police had to be called to restore order.

At this time waterlogging caused another accident when Martinet HN961 became bogged down during its take off run resulting in damage to the propeller, wings and undercarriage.

Reorganisation during 1943 resulted in the disbandment of Army Co-operation Command and its absorbtion into Fighter Command, which took over responsibility for the airfield in June. Following further changes, in December 1605 Flight combined with 1628 Flight to form 631 Squadron. This unit continued to use Henleys for target towing long after other similar squadrons had been re-equipped with purpose built Martinets.

On 20th February 1944 Henley L3325 caught fire in the air and was subsequently ditched in the sea a few hundred yards from shore, two miles south of the airfield, its crew being picked up by launch, both men suffering from the effects of immersion and shock. An Army unit based nearby, the RASC's No.1 Amphibious Training Wing (then training with DUKWs for the June 'D' Day landings) sought permission to recover the Henley and on the 21st they successfully brought the aircraft ashore.

During this period every branch of the armed forces had a training unit of some kind based in the locality, much of their effort being directed towards the coming invasion of Europe by the Allies in June. The number of servicemen in and around Tywyn was estimated to be in excess of six thousand.

Station strength during February 1944 was 16 Officers, 25 NCOs and 185 Airmen. Flying hours achieved during the month on army co-operation and target towing duties amounted to 334 hours, which was average for 631 Squadron at this time.

In March the squadron took delivery of two Hurricanes, thereby allowing gun laying practice to take place, whilst some of the Henleys were withdrawn from service, to be replaced by Martinets. Nine of these aircraft were on strength by September 1944, with familiarisation and training flights pushing up monthly flying hours to a total of 366 hours. At the end of December the squadron had 21 aircraft — eight Henleys, nine Martinets, two Hurricanes, an Oxford and a Tiger Moth hack.

During March 1944 the pilots had a welcome break from monotonous army co-operation flying and target towing when they found themselves, in company with nine pilots from Llanbedr, taking part in an 'escaping prisoners' exercise.

Dressed in blue overalls and wearing a red armband the pilots were to act as escaping prisoners, and after being driven by lorry to a distance of some twelve miles away from Tywyn they were then set the task of returning without being stopped by the Home Guard.

A time limit of five hours was imposed, use of the English language was not permitted, no vehicles were to be taken, no violence was to be used and each man was to carry no more than 4d (about 2 pence) to be used for telephone calls if in real difficulty. Of the eighteen pilots that took part only one succeeded in reaching Tywyn, all the others being intercepted at various points although several managed to evade capture until the last moment.

On 3rd March the AOC of No.70 Group visited the airfield. The station record book notes the visit and points to what appears to have been a long standing problem — "The Air Commodore, after inspecting, dining and staying the night brought up the paucity of lavatory rolls. This subject has been referred to in every sanitary inspection to date"!

An impression of the life of a target towing pilot during this period is provided by Bert Pudney, who began his RAF career in 1937 at the age of 16 as an apprentice armourer. He was accepted for pilot training in 1939 but was informed there would be a long wait before he could start training and so he continued as an armourer, serving with a number of squadrons including No.65, where, during the first weeks of the Battle of Britain he was responsible for the Spitfire of Stanford Tuck.

Then in late 1942 came the eagerly awaited posting to Rhodesia for pilot training. After gaining his wings Bert returned to the UK, where, after a conversion course to Blenheims, then reverting back to single engined flying he was told there were no immediate vacancies in fighter squadrons but he would be given useful work while waiting his turn, which would probably be after the invasion of Europe. In May 1944, with the rank of Sergeant, he found himself at Tywyn.

"I was soon put to work", he writes, "and after the regulation five hours solo in Henleys I started to tow targets. There were several kinds of target, the largest being a red flag 40 feet long and 6 feet wide which was towed at various heights at a distance of 2,000 feet from the beach at Tonfanau, where Royal Artillery units had their guns — 4.5s and 3.7s.

"We towed at 140 m.p.h. because anything faster would send engine temperatures up. Some of the shelling was erratic, sometimes the target was hit and it dropped into the sea, sometimes the wire was cut and we lost the flag but quite often the RA gunners seemed to be aiming at me and not the flag. I remember my Target Towing Operator (TTO) once saying after a few shots surrounded us, 'This is getting bloody dangerous, Skipper!'

"At the same time, the Army was training to operate radar and do ranging work for the guns. We aircrew believed that they would range on the first blip they saw on the screen instead of waiting for the second blip, which was of course, the target. So if things got a bit hot around us we would radio down to the Army Control and inform them that we were pulling the target and not pushing it.

"We also used a variety of drogues, carrying about a dozen or so then streaming them with about 400 feet of tow for various bodies to shoot at, e.g. RAF Regiment, Commandos etc. Their bullets were dipped in various coloured paints and after a few passes the drogue was dropped to check which groups had hit the target. This was indicated, of course, by the coloured holes in the white nylon.

"We also had various silent routines, i.e. no gunfire or tow, just gun laying practice or radar calibration. Another exercise in which we were involved was called 'Submarine Simulation'. In this we towed a white drogue on about 50 feet of cable, very low and in fact hedge hopping, approaching from inland at about 180 m.p.h., aiming to pass over the line of guns on the promenade at right angles, heading out to sea. After 25 seconds (approx. 2,000 yards) and at sea level we cut the tow and got the hell out of it with a rate 4 vertical bank turn because by that time the first shells were on their way!

"The drogue, after being cut, would float on the sea and be a target for the gunners to shoot at. I think this was for the training of RA gunners who manned the big old guns installed in the stern of merchant ships in those days.

"In the early days we had a Hurricane on charge which was used for radar calibration etc. Later on we got a few Spitfire Vs and simulated 'Flying Bomb' attacks. This consisted of approaching from inland in a shallow dive at full throttle aiming to pass over the guns and out to sea at approx. 2,000 feet and as fast as one could go. When we got a few Spitfire XVIs I was able to work up a speed of well over 400 m.p.h.

"Apart from our own squadron workload, we sometimes went to help out other units, at Bodorgan for instance, took Army types to meetings and conferences etc., gave flights in our aircraft to ATC cadets and more than once had to divert from army co-operation to go and look for a stray B-17 or Liberator in the Irish Sea.

"The Squadron started off with Henleys, then these were replaced by Martinets, which did not make much of an impression on me, and finally the Vultee Vengeance which was a smasher although operating this type meant we had to move to Llanbedr, which had runways.

"One day I was about to land at Llanbedr after a target towing flight when control asked me to investigate a suspected crash. I soon found the wreckage of an aircraft burning furiously on the sandy beach just to the north of Harlech Castle, [This was Mosquito NT221, from No.8 OTU, which made a forced landing on Harlech beach on 20th February 1945 after an engine caught fire. The aircraft burst into flames after striking sand dunes and the pilot died from his injuries.]

"I must also mention the terrible weather in which we, in 631 Squadron, flew when it seemed the rest of the RAF was grounded. Even with the cloudbase down to 400 feet we still went out to do figure of eight courses for the Bofors guns along the nearby beach!"

Bert Pudney was eventually commissioned and was the squadron adjutant of 631 when the war ended.

After the 'D' Day landings of June 1944, to which all the training of many army units near Tywyn had been leading up, the army co-operation duties of 631 Squadron lessened somewhat, with the monthly total of flying hours down to 280.

On 8th July probably the largest aircraft ever to do so landed at Tywyn. This was a B-17, serial 42-31321, of the USAAF's 390th Bomb Group returning from North Africa. After encountering bad weather the aircraft became lost and the pilot, 1st Lt. J. Ratcliffe, found himself in a rather unenviable position flying along the Welsh coast in worsening weather and with little fuel left. He decided to land at Tywyn but the airfield was far too small for such an aircraft — it ran across an adjoining railway line and collided with an air raid shelter. A fire started in the starboard wing which was quickly extinguished by the RAF fire tender with assistance from the local Fire Brigade. None of the B-17's fifteen occupants suffered any injuries but the aircraft was a write off and was later removed by an USAAF party.

In October 1944 the airfield became badly waterlogged yet again, which forced 631's Martinets to move to Llanbedr for a few days. They also lost Henley L3296 on the 15th when it made a belly landing and as a result was damaged beyond repair.

Further losses occurred during February 1945 when two of the squadron's aircraft crashed, both piloted by the same man. The first was a Hurricane which overshot on landing and ran into the railway line, resulting in Cat. E damage. It was flown by a New Zealander, Pilot Officer H. H. Russell. On 28th February he was also the pilot of a Henley which crashed in the Dysynni estuary near the airfield. He did not survive this second accident.

At the time the war was ending 631 received further replacements in the form of Vengeances and Spitfires, already referred to by Bert Pudney, but as no post-war use of Tywyn was intended the squadron transferred to Llanbedr in May 1945.

No.22 Group, Technical Training Command took over in May but two months later, on 25th July, Tywyn was closed. Subsequently it was transferred to the War Office and became an army camp and adventure school whilst the landing ground was turned into a sports field.

Chapter 9

New Use for Old Quarries
Hunting Aviation Ltd. & 31 MU, Dinorwig

Perhaps the most important industrial development in Gwynedd during the nineteenth and early twentieth century was that of slate quarrying, which had a profound effect upon both landscape and people.

Slates of every shape and size were shipped in countless numbers to all parts of the world. Some quarries became very large, creating huge workings which bit deep into mountainsides and radically altered the environment as a result.

One such example was the vast Dinorwig quarry at Llanberis. At the beginning of the war part of this quarry was requisitioned by the Ministry of Aircraft Production for aircraft component manufacture, carried out by the firm of Hunting Aviation Ltd. Also, the RAF used it as a bomb storage depot.

Although not directly concerned with operational flying as such, the story of Dinorwig's contribution to the war effort is, nevertheless, worth relating, albeit in very brief form.

On 15th August 1940 Hunting Aviation's factory at Croydon was badly damaged by bombing, bringing important production to a halt. The MAP quickly requisitioned other temporary sites at Epsom and Ewell but Lord Beaverbrook, as Minister, insisted with his customary forcefulness, that a permanent location had to be found in a 'safe' area with the minimum of delay. North Wales was such an area where a number of localities existed for possible relocation, but which was the most suitable? This was the question facing company chairman Sir Percy Hunting.

In the event, Gwynedd was chosen through the combined influence of Beaverbrook and Lloyd George. Beaverbrook wanted production restarted as soon as possible and Lloyd George, with whom Sir Percy was friendly, wanted to secure a boost for the local economy, which the relocated factory would undoubtedly provide.

Duly, Sir Percy accompanied by W. A. Summers, works manager at Croydon, travelled to Caernarfon where they met Lloyd George and Goronwy Owen, the local MP. Following a tour of the area two sites were selected — firstly, Peblig Mill on the outskirts of Caernarfon, and secondly, Dinorwig Slate Quarry. Hunting took over these sites on 28th August 1940 but only forty staff members, headed by W. A. Summers, actually moved to North Wales. Their first job was to recruit and train local labour. A training school was started at Caernarfon enabling the workforce to build up fairly quickly at the rate of 100 or so every month. In two years 3,000 people, mostly from Gwynedd, were employed by the company.

The first components were delivered from the factory in November 1940. Amongst the items manufactured were Wellington and Halifax components, Stirling bomb bays and centre sections, Defiant wings and Lancaster front fuselage sections, completely equipped.

The company also had a change of name after moving to Gwynedd. It was known as Necaco Ltd. — North East Coast Aircraft Company. This seemingly inappropriate and slightly puzzling name for a company based at the bottom of a mountain in North Wales was dreamt up by Sir Percy Hunting in an effort to mislead German intelligence and ensure his factory did not get bombed twice!

In the event Sir Percy had no further problems with German bombers but plenty arose from Hunting's relationship with the Vaynol Estate, owners of Dinorwig. From the start, requisitioning of the quarry had been resented by the owners and many bitter disputes arose, for instance over Hunting's plan to expand their factory. At first they had the use of two large slate-finishing sheds and a deep tunnel (which previously had been turned down by the National Gallery for storage of the nation's art treasures in favour of Manod Quarry at Blaenau Ffestiniog) but in order to meet expansion targets further buildings were requisitioned at the end of 1941.

Legal wrangles resulted, which became quite acrimonious. However, given the circumstances of war and the Government's sweeping powers there was little that the Vaynol estate could do to prevent the planned expansion from taking place.

Attitudes were revealed in this candid remark by one solicitor to another, on the opposite side of the dispute, "I am afraid that in that part of Wales they have had such a peaceful time that they have not realised the importance of this aircraft manufacture but I expect you in London like ourselves near Merseyside [he was writing from Chester] have realised it to the full."

In February 1942 the MAP Directorate of Camouflage ordered that the Dinorwig site had to be camouflaged by the end of March. It was a decision which caused further argument as the quarry owners, to their dismay, found that they had to pay half the cost! The Government paid the other half but apparently Hunting did not have to pay at all, which from the Vaynol Estate's point of view seemed manifestly unjust and did nothing but add insult to injury.

At the end of the war the components manufactured here became surplus and it is rumoured that items left after closure were simply thrown into nearby Lake Padarn. Although this site was abandoned in 1945 Hunting remained at their Caernarfon factory and thus provided some continuation of employment by manufacturing metal furniture. This venture ended in 1947 because of increasing difficulties in obtaining raw material.

Brief reference must also be made to the firm of Daimler, who moved to Bangor in order to produce aero-engine components. They employed over 1,000 people at one stage, giving yet another boost to the local economy. Daimler ceased production after the war ended but happily the factory remained and is still providing employment today manufacturing telephone and electrical equipment. It is, at present, owned by the Ferranti Group.

The other wartime user of quarries at Llanberis was No.31 Maintenance Unit of the RAF. This unit was established in May 1941 as a storage depot for bombs and explosives. The chosen site, on the southern side of Lake Padarn, was ideal for its purpose with the deep holes made by quarrying providing excellent storage for bombs.

On 2nd June the unit opened officially, with Wing Commander R. Horstmann as CO and on the following day the first consignment of bombs arrived — ten truck loads from RAF Swynnerton. By the end of the month 1,837 tons of bombs had been received and stored.

During the following months every available space seems to have been used to store explosives, with a number of dispersed sites coming into operation, e.g. at the hamlets of Rhiwlas and Clwt-y-Bont. From these stores operational RAF units were supplied with the hardware necessary for them to continue their operations.

The task of receiving, storing and issuing bombs, high explosives, incendiaries etc. was carried out without interruption by 31 MU for the rest of the war, with a workforce of 500 men, many of whom were local civilians.

Perhaps the most memorable incident took place soon after the unit had been established. Not far from the railway line into Llanberis a large subterranean area had been created, with three floors. To make it bomb proof a thick layer of concrete had been placed over this underground building but unfortunately there was insufficient structural strength to support the weight of concrete.

An alert worker noticed cracks suddenly appearing in the roof one day and raised the alarm. All employees were immediately evacuated and twenty minutes later the roof collapsed.

When the war ended large stocks of explosives were stored at Llanberis where they remained for many years until eventually it was decided to dispose of them. For instance, in December 1949 the unit's entire stock of incendiary bombs, some 4,500 tons, were deemed to have become unusable because of prolonged storage in the open and it was decided to destroy them. Destruction was carried out on site at the rate of 60-70 bombs per day. The unit continued in existence throughout the 1950s though with a much reduced workforce. When all bombs and explosives had been disposed of, 31 MU finally closed down.

In subsequent years little use was made of the site except by the C.E.G.B. when constructing the Dinorwig Pumped Storage Power Station.

Chapter 10

Catalina Contract
The Work of Saunders-Roe Ltd., Beaumaris

There exists a short piece of film, shot during the war by a local amateur cameraman, depicting activity on the Menai Straits. After showing a number of marine craft, Motor Torpedo Boats, RAF air sea rescue launches etc. the sequence ends with views of elegant looking flying boats moored off Beaumaris. They were American built Catalinas, ferried from the US to Gwynedd, where the firm of Saunders-Roe, based at Beaumaris, converted over three hundred of these machines to meet RAF operational requirements.

In 1940 German air raids on the firm's headquarters and factory at Cowes, Isle of Wight, were causing great disruption, making it difficult and dangerous to work with any degree of efficiency. They, in common with other aircraft manufacturers were thus forced to move to safer areas well away from southern England. Vickers Supermarine, for instance, moved from Southampton to the Clyde, and Shorts from Rochester to Windermere in the Lake District.

For Saunders-Roe the problem was to locate a suitable area and so a small team led by test pilot Leslie Ash went north in search of sites. As builders of flying boats they needed, primarily, an area of deep and sheltered water but the team experienced difficulty in locating a good site that had not already been occupied by a military unit of one kind or another. Eventually they arrived in North Wales where the Conwy estuary seemed promising. However, because extensive mud flats were exposed at low tide this site was rejected.

The team then moved to Anglesey and investigated the Menai Straits, concentrating on the eastern end. At Beaumaris they found adequately deep and sheltered water stretching for a distance of four miles to Menai Bridge. Furthermore, as the Straits ran in a south west/north east direction, parallel with the prevailing winds, the maximum length of water would nearly always be available for take-off and landing. In addition, no military airfields existed nearby, thus allowing Saunders-Roe complete freedom of the local airspace.

Beaumaris' suitability could not be doubted when Ash and his colleagues found a large house known as 'Friars' for sale, together with 50 acres of land, on the waterfront one mile from the town. Hangars and buildings could easily be erected on the land and a slipway built down to the water. Also, as the house was empty the unpleasantness of forcing occupants to leave did not arise, thereby eschewing the nasty side of requisitioning, in this case at least. It was an ideal site.

In October 1940 the design department moved to Anglesey. One of the first tasks was to study drawings of an American flying boat, the Consolidated PBY-5 which the Ministry of Aircraft Production proposed to buy in quantity for use by Coastal Command on anti-submarine patrols. The department studied these drawings at the request of the Ministry, who thought modifications were necessary before the PBY could enter service. Saunders-Roe agreed with this view.

At the Ministry, a special section, the Directorate of Production, Canadian and American, (DPCA), came into being to organise and supervise work on this aircraft type and a number of others also. Needless to say they maintained close contact with Saunders-Roe at all times.

In December 1940 one point under discussion was the choice of name for the PBY-5 when in RAF service — 'Plymouth' was thought suitable but eventually 'Catalina' was agreed upon. This was the name of the sea area and island off San Diego, USA, where the flying boat was manufactured.

By January 1941 the RAF's shortage of flying boats for anti-submarine patrol had become so critical that special arrangements took place at the highest level of government in Britain and America in order to initiate the Catalina programme without delay. Seven PBYs of the US Navy were to be sent to the UK for trials, the first of which arrived in mid-January at the Marine Aircraft Experimental Establishment, Helensburgh, where it was closely inspected by Saunders-Roe engineers, amongst others. Some forty modifications were suggested to allow RAF operational use but the MAP halved this figure on the grounds of urgency. The actual job of modification was intended to be carried out by Scottish Aviation at Greenock, with design of the necessary modifications taking place at Beaumaris but such was the urgency that a design team left Anglesey to work directly on site at Greenock.

Some of the changes, for example, were to radio sets, instrumentation and hull modifications to allow stowage of RAF equipment. Enormous pressure was being exerted by the MAP who wanted all design work completed in three weeks. Thanks to Herculean efforts by Saunders-Roe staff it took seventeen days.

The Ministry then kept up pressure for conversion of the Catalinas to begin as quickly as possible but problems soon became evident at Greenock — lack of proper facilities, materials and tools. Also, work had to be done in the open and to make matters worse Scottish Aviation had few staff experienced in dealing with flying boats. Afraid that this company, in consequence, would not be able to handle the expected volume of work the Ministry requested Saunders-Roe to make arrangements for similar work to be done at their Anglesey site. As already mentioned, spare land and sheltered water permitted this development although the company was somewhat unprepared when the request was made.

With no technical staff or hangars and only a half-finished slipway Saunders-Roe had little time in which to organise the conversion operation before the first Catalinas, two in number, arrived in April 1941. At the beginning, work was carried out on the aircraft when they were afloat. This situation was clearly unsatisfactory but after completion of the slipway the first Catalina, serial AM266, was hauled ashore on 28th April.

Providing sufficient storage space for materials etc. presented many difficulties. All manner of unlikely places in and around Friars were hastily pressed into service. The stables of Bryn Hyfryd, a large house nearby became the Embodiment Loan Store and loose equipment removed from aircraft on arrival was stored in the pavilion at the end of Beaumaris pier! These scatterings inevitably resulted in wasted time and inefficiency until construction of hangars and stores at Friars itself eventually resolved the problem.

Space was also critically short for another manufacturing commitment, which it was decided to carry out during this period — the construction of wooden hulls for the Supermarine Walrus Mk.II ASR amphibian. Almost any kind of available buildings were utilised, from garages to garden sheds, not only in Beaumaris but also Menai Bridge and even Bangor.

During August 1941 a hangar was dismantled at Cowes and rebuilt at Beaumaris, thus providing much needed space. Rapid expansion of staff also followed, many of whom were recruited locally. Hardly anyone in this category possessed engineering skills and so they had to be taught by the company. More space became available in December 1941 when the MAP provided a T2 hangar. Thereafter hangar and workshop space grew steadily to keep pace with the increasing number of Catalinas and other aircraft types being dealt with.

In charge at Beaumaris throughout the war was Harry Broadsmith, a quiet and unassuming man who nevertheless proved a popular and successful manager. Other key staff members included tall and charming Henry Knowler, the chief designer, and test pilot Leslie Ash.

After the first two Catalinas arrived in April the numbers of aircraft received subsequently for conversion remained small. Only ten were converted during the remainder of 1941. The RAF's requirements were not being met and towards the autumn, as the situation became increasingly critical, pressure was again exerted to increase the flow of aircraft from the United States.

One way of achieving this objective was through the military and diplomatic contacts of the RAF delegation in Washington, who in October were informed by the Air Ministry that 77 Catalinas were needed by April 1942. Consolidated readily answered British calls for help, so that during 1942 the numbers of flying boats sent to Britain increased rapidly. In fact Saunders-Roe converted 63 that year, a fivefold increase over the previous twelve months.

The Catalinas which arrived in Anglesey were ferried across the Atlantic, usually from Goose Bay in Canada. At first ferry crews were civilians, a motley bunch of adventurers who undertook the arduous and risky flight as much for the devilment of it as anything else. Later, when America came into the war military crews took over.

After arrival the aircraft, laden with spares, munitions of war and more often than not, contraband, were moored in the Menai Straits. As originally envisaged this stretch of water provided sheltered moorings extending from Friars to Menai Bridge, four miles away. Sometimes as many as ten or twelve Catalinas could be seen on the Straits. Locating a mooring was not done at random however. Something akin to a queue system was operated, whereby new arrivals found themselves at the end of the queue near Glyn Garth or Menai Bridge and aircraft about to be taken ashore for conversion or ready for departure were moored nearer to the factory site.

Assistance was provided during mooring operations by motor launch, which then took the Catalina's crew ashore. Interestingly enough, one of these launches was skippered by Winifred Brown, a well known aviatrix of the 1930s. She became the first woman to win the King's Cup Air Race in 1930 and had already visited Gwynedd that same year when taking part in the Llandudno Flying Week. Subsequently she gave up flying and turned to boats instead.

In 1940 she and her husband, wishing to be secure from German air raids, moved from Manchester to Anglesey, which she described as: "A safe area where food abounded, and pigs and chickens disappear overnight and milk appeared as farm butter — off ration!"

Living in Beaumaris when Saunders-Roe came to the area she was delighted to find an old friend, Harry Broadsmith, in charge. They had first met in Australia in 1927 and now, as their paths had crossed once again, Broadsmith immediately offered her a job with the company. Her duties mostly were to transport crews to and from moored Catalinas, and the towing of flying boats, a difficult job calling for good seamanship.

Winifred Brown had a remarkable personality, as competitive and assertive as any male yet not lacking in feminine sensibility and other attributes of her sex. She eventually became marine superintendent at Friars.

For the launch crews one advantage of their job was the opportunity to acquire contraband from the Americans, besides left-overs from food rations such as oranges and bananas, which would casually be thrown away. Another group of workers who looked forward to 'pickings' were those responsible for clearing the Catalinas of loose equipment prior to the start of conversion work. A forgotten packet of cigarettes or bar of chocolate could usually be found somewhere within the aircraft's hull!

If space was not immediately available ashore to store the flying boats they had to remain at their moorings, sometimes for lengthy periods. The engines would then have to be run every seven days. As it was not possible or permissible to run engines whilst moored the Catalinas therefore had to be taxied, a job done by qualified aircrew only. Aircraft left in the water for three weeks or longer, however, would soon get into bad shape.

When hangar space became avilable the flying boats were towed by launch and made fast at an inshore buoy close to the slipway. A beaching party wearing wading suits then had to attach a wheeled trolley allowing the Catalinas to be hauled tail first up the slipway and across a public road into the factory grounds.

The men who did this job had a difficult time, struggling chest high in water with the heavy trolley. Often waves completely swamped the party but they did have some rewards — a few extra shillings in their pay packets for each aircraft handled plus a generous measure of hard earned rum every time they went into the water. This was certainly true in the case of one man known as Dic Bâch (little Richard) whose name accurately reflected his lack of stature and therefore, it would be reasonable to conclude, also his intrinsic unsuitability for work of this nature. Whatever the apparent shortcomings in the logic of the situation the poor man frequently found himself in danger of being totally submerged and had to add inches-thick wooden soles to his boots in order, literally, to keep his head above water!

The first priority once ashore was to wash the aircraft down with fresh water. Then all loose equipment was removed, after which conversion work could begin. The extent and nature of conversion did not remain static but changed continually throughout the war, depending upon a host of variables, e.g. aircraft Mark, RAF suggestions, urgency of requirements and continuing research by the MAP and RAE Farnborough. Generally, changes were made to radio sets, instrumentation, fitment of a British type compass and hull alterations to allow stowage of British equipment. Also, US bomb racks had to be exchanged for a British design in order that a heavier bomb load could be carried.

An important piece of equipment installed in the Catalinas during 1941 was a form of airborne radar known as ASV. By the year's end a more powerful version had been developed — Long Range Air Surface Vessel (LRASV). Installation trials were carried out locally on Catalina JX215 which arrived in June 1941. It was used subsequently to test all RAF/MAP initiated modifications in addition to providing an airborne trials facility for technical developments by RAE scientists.

Details of the new radar remained a closely guarded secret and so whenever Farnborough and RAF personnel conducted flight trials the equipment they brought with them remained firmly hidden from view. Saunders-Roe's responsibility was for the aerial installation and its structural integrity within the wing. Company engineers, when present on a test flight, were physically prevented by screens from observing the radar set.

This long range radar, which promised to be a vital tool in the search for enemy submarines, had the highest priority. Even before installation trials were complete the MAP urged Saunders-Roe to prepare drawings and advance information in order that Consolidated could incorporate the radar in aircraft before delivery to the UK. The first Catalina with LRASV already installed arrived at Beaumaris in July 1942. Also, from that time onwards aircraft were received under the Lend/Lease Act which allowed the supply of munitions to Britain on a massive scale, at American expense.

Another piece of equipment installed in Catalinas was the Leigh Light, which necessitated some wing strengthening. This powerful light enabled night operations to take place. Increased armament was also fitted usually by adding another machine-gun to the one already positioned in the flying boat's bow.

After completion of conversion work and inspection, loose equipment was reloaded, the compass swung and the flying boat relaunched. Every Catalina was then test flown by Les Ash or an RAF crew specially attached to Saunders-Roe for the purpose, before being delivered to Coastal Command squadrons.

Accidents to the flying boats at Beaumaris were fortunately very rare. One ran aground on a sand bank after being tested and tipped up on its nose, causing damage to the chine and slight injury to a crewman. Another, FP127, broke its mooring at night in December 1942 and drifted away, unseen, at the mercy of wind and water past Puffin Island and out into the Irish Sea. It was observed the following morning in Liverpool Bay where a Royal Navy vessel took it in tow. Before reaching Liverpool, however, the Catalina sank, probably through inexpert towing. Following this incident modifications to the mooring system were introduced and no further losses occurred.

One interesting Catalina seen locally in 1944 was ex-BOAC G-AGBJ 'Guba'. Built in 1937 it had been used for a variety of purposes including the selection of Indian Ocean bases for the RAF, had flown around the world, and from 1941 had been used by BOAC on the Poole-Lisbon-Lagos route. Its last operational flight with BOAC was in April 1943 after which it received an RAF serial, SM706, and was transferred to Saunders-Roe who used it for testing moorings in the Menai Straits. Sometime in 1944, with its useful life over, this historic aircraft was scuttled off Pwllheli.

There were seven Marks of Catalina — I, Ib, II, IIa, III, IVa and IVb. The Mark I was the basic PBY-5 flying boat of which 29 were converted between June 1941 and April 1943. When aircraft were received under the Lend/Lease scheme they were designated Ib — 75 were converted between July 1942 and July 1943. The Mark II and IIa were special allotments of US Navy and RCAF aircraft. Only 12 were converted — 2 Mk.IIs in April 1941 and 10 Mk.IIas in 1942. The first amphibian Mk.III arrived in April 1942 under an extremely urgent conversion programme which rapidly faltered when it was found that the presence of a chassis meant such a complete re-arrangement of equipment inside the hull that it was impossible to complete the conversion schedule within the allotted time. Only six aircraft were converted and they were relegated to training roles. Subsequently the chassis was removed and the aircraft became flying boats, pure and simple.

The majority of Catalinas converted were Mark IVs, both 'a' and 'b', ('a' manufactured by Consolidated in the US and 'b' by Boeing in Canada). Over 150 were dealt with by Saunders-Roe, the first in May 1943. This Mark was similar to the Mark I except for a new aerial system and provision for US bombs and bomb racks only. Over three hundred Catalinas were converted to meet RAF requirements by Saunders-Roe between 1941 and 1945. Broken down into totals by year and Mark the figures are:-

Year		Mark	
1941 —	12 aircraft	Mark I —	29
1942 —	63 aircraft	Mark Ib —	75
1943 —	70 aircraft	Mark II —	2
1944 —	114 aircraft	Mark IIa —	10
1945 —	37+ aircraft	Mark III —	6
		Mark IVa —	43
		Mark IVb —	113
		(plus 32 Mark IVs retrospectively)	
Total	—300+	Total	— 310

Slightly annoying was the unevenness in the flow of lying boats arriving at Beaumaris. With wide fluctuations, twelve aircraft in November 1942 for instance but only two in December, staff were either over extended or did not have enough to do. At times the management found it difficult to ensure a steady input of work for staff.

When a particularly urgent requirement arose, such as the installation of airborne radar, the workforce would co-operate fully to get the job done as quickly as possible. Frequently the MAP, under Lord Beaverbrook's dynamic leadership, would exert great pressure from the highest levels within the Ministry in order to achieve the maximum effort. Beaverbrook himself would often telephone Harry Broadsmith urging all possible haste in the design of some new installation or delivery of badly needed Catalinas. In fact Broadsmith received the Minister's personal thanks in this undated note:

> Dear Mr Broadsmith,
>
> Your activities in connection with the Catalina aircraft have been of immense benefit to the country. The speedy conversion of this type of aircraft to operational use was, and remains, a vital necessity. It constitutes a major achievement in the Battle of the Atlantic and I take this opportunity of sending you my warm thanks for all you have done.
>
> (signed) Beaverbrook

In December 1944, when the threat from U-boats had lessened, the possibility of employing Catalinas in other roles besides anti-submarine patrol arose. Air Sea Rescue seemed obvious and Saunders-Roe was asked to prepare a RATOG design which would make the flying boats suitable for this role. A trial installation was constructed and attached to the MAP DTD aircraft, JX215, at Beaumaris. Also, early in 1945 with ASR duties still in mind, the firm was asked to convert a squadron of Mark IVs enabling them to carry an airborne lifeboat. But with the end of the war imminent neither RATOG nor ASR lifeboat projects ever went beyond a few trial installations.

Although the Catalina will always be the aircraft associated with Beaumaris, other types manufactured in the United States were also dealt with but on a much smaller scale. These were the Kingfisher, Coronado, Seamew, and Mariner.

The first, received in May 1942, was the Vought-Sikorsky Kingfisher, a two seater low wing monoplane intended for the Fleet Air Arm as a reconnaisance aircraft. It was provided with a chassis which could be fitted to allow use either as a seaplane or landplane. One Kingfisher, FN660, was allocated by the MAP to Friars for testing of proposed modifications but only a few were converted locally as the Catalina programme had priority. Most were converted either by Saunders-Roe working parties at RNAS stations or Scottish Aviation at Greenock.

Another type to receive attention was the largely unsuccessful Consolidated Coronado. Not unlike a four engined version of the Catalina, with similar wing tip extendable floats, this aircraft, unfortunately, suffered from design faults and failure by the manufacturer to deal effectively with development troubles. It lacked range, was too heavy, and at the same time structurally weak.

The first Coronado, JX470, arrived in this country from the United States in April 1943 and was flown from the Scottish Aviation site at Largs to Anglesey on the 29th. It was the largest aircraft so far dealt with at Friars. Shortly after, it was decided to send the Coronado to MAEE Helensburgh for trials but a mishap during take off temporarily halted this plan. The port wing tip float was retracted prematurely resulting in a dipped wing which actually touched the water. Before complete disaster happened the float was hastily re-extended, thus minimising damage. The flying boat was run aground on a sandbank, with its wing dug in the sand until it was refloated on a rising tide. Damage had been caused to some wing panels, the float and float motor, which burnt out after its emergency use. The flying boat eventually reached Helensburgh on 14th May.

Two more Coronados, JX495 and JX496, arrived in Britain during August, JX495 being sent to the MAEE and the other to RAF Greenock, at which station a conference was held in September on the future use of the type. Because of the shortcomings already mentioned Coastal Command decided against the Coronado, suggesting that perhaps Transport Command might be able to find a suitable role for it.

However, Transport Command was equally unenthusiastic and decided to reject the Coronado also. With an uncertain future ahead JX496 was flown to Beaumaris for further trials, which in the event, did not take place. Then in October 1943 BOAC was offered JX495 for a short period in order to carry out evaluation tests at Hythe. Soon the aircraft was back in Anglesey because of leaking fuel tanks, caused by poor workmanship and inferior materials.

A further period of trials with JX496 did little to convince BOAC that they should take the Coronado. On the contrary, they were fully aware of its defects and wanted nothing more to do with the project. Clearly the Coronado was an unwanted flying boat but what was to be done with it?

In an attempt to resolve the question Transport Command was approached for a second time and asked to reconsider its original, unfavourable opinion of the aircraft. Pending firm decisions the trial Coronados were stored afloat at Beaumaris. Eventually, in January 1944 JX495 went to MAEE Helensburgh and JX496 to 57MU, Wig Bay, in September of the same year. After further trials the type finally entered service in limited numbers with a somewhat reluctant Transport Command, which operated ten of these machines on transatlantic flights between Canada, Iceland and Scotland.

Perhaps an even more unsuccessful type was the Curtiss Seamew, a two seater capable of conversion to either sea or land use but unfortunately it was a very heavy and under-powered aircraft. Because of this drawback it offered limited operational capabilities only and ended up as a minor trainer in the use of radio equipment. The only example seen at Beaumaris arrived by road in May 1943 from Mona, to where it had been flown from Boscombe Down before being partially dismantled for the last part of its journey.

Another American type was the Martin Mariner, a gull-winged general reconnaisance flying boat. The first arrived in Anglesey in August 1943 and was then sent to Helensburgh early in September for flight and water handling trials. In October and November further examples arrived and a requisition was received for six to be modified for use by 524 Squadron, Coastal Command. However, in December, when work on a further six was in hand, the project was abruptly halted by the MAP with instructions that the aircraft were to go into storage. No explanation was given but it was believed to be due to excessive fire risks from the fuel tanks positioned under the flight deck. During 1944 22 Mariners out of the 26 delivered to the UK were ferried back to the United States.

The year 1944 also saw some interesting flight testing at Beaumaris of the Spitfire in unusual form — with floats. This idea had been developed to allow operations in areas of rugged terrain where airfields did not exist. Five aircraft had floats attached, one in April 1940, another in September 1941, two more in August 1942 and the last during the summer of 1944.

The latter machine, a Mk.IX, MJ892, received conversion to floatplane by Folland Aircraft of Hamble, the intention being to use this version in the Pacific.

The aircraft was sent to Saunders-Roe for handling trials and was first flown at Beaumaris on 19th June 1944 with Jeffrey Quill at the controls. But soon after the test programme started it was decided that no operational requirement existed for a fighter floatplane because of the changing circumstances of the war and the project was consequently brought to an end. Spitfire MJ892 left in September 1944 and was re-converted to a landplane. Of the five Spitfire floatplanes none ever saw operational use.

Also in 1944 a floatplane version of the Auster Mk.V briefly received flight testing locally before being transferred to Helensburgh for full trials. This was TJ207, fitted with 'Queen Bee' type floats and was in fact the very first Auster floatplane.

Then in September 1949, long after aviation activity had ended at Beaumaris, another Auster Mk.V floatplane made an appearance. This particular machine was registered VP-FAC, (ex-TW476), and was intended for use in the Falkland Islands and Antarctic regions. The aircraft was flown by Auster's test pilot, Les Leetham, and amongst the observers at Friars were R. E. Bird, the company chief designer, F. Elliott, secretary to the Governor of the Falkland Islands, and E. Hill of the British Antarctic Survey. In October the Auster was crated and shipped to its destination where in June 1955 it was scrapped because of corrosion.

But to turn now to Saunders-Roe's own projects: before war broke out the company, along with its competitors, Short Bros. and Supermarine, produced design studies in response to Air Ministry specifications. One such was Specification R5/39, intended as a replacement for the Sunderland. In February 1939 Saunders-Roe decided to build a half scale model of their R5/39 design, for research into the various aspects of flying boat behaviour. With the prolific Henry Knowler in charge of this project the result was a most attractive two seater 'mini' flying boat of 50' wingspan, powered by four Pobjoy 95 h.p. engines.

Registered G-AFZS and designated the Saro A.37 it was better known as the 'Shrimp' for obvious reasons. It first flew in October 1939 at Cowes but was transferred to Beaumaris in 1940. In between testing Catalinas Les Ash usually flew this aircraft.

By 1940 the Air Ministry R5/39 project had been cancelled as no replacement was thought necessary for the Sunderland. Official thinking was not clear or decisive on flying boat policy in general but nonetheless

Saunders-Roe continued to produce design studies on their own initiative.

For example, Saro S.42, submitted to the Air Ministry in July 1942, proposed joining the Lancaster wing and engines to a hull based on research with the Shrimp, which had rapidly proved itself a most valuable research vehicle. But the Air Ministry expressed no interest in these ideas. Favour was being given to land based aircraft and indeed to some extent the writing was already on the wall for flying boat manufacturers.

However, the company found some solace by being asked to join Short Bros. in the development of a large scale, long range version of the Sunderland, to be known as the Shetland. Design of the wings and engine installation now became Saunders-Roe's responsibility and a wind tunnel was specially built at Beaumaris for wing testing.

Then in June 1943 doubts arose at the Air Ministry over the advisability of allowing work on the Shetland to continue, but to Saunders-Roe's relief outright cancellation was avoided. The Ministry decision was something of a compromise — construction could continue but henceforth the Shetland was to be a transport aircraft only.

Whilst Air Ministry priorities wavered, the Shrimp was providing valuable test data. Early in 1944 it received further modification when the twin tail was removed and a scaled down Shetland fin and rudder fitted. In April tests of the Shetland wing tip floats and elevators were undertaken. These tests proved successful as the Shrimp was found to be very stable. At this time it was taken on charge by the MAP and given the serial TK580. After a most useful life this little aircraft was eventually scrapped in 1949.

As for the Shetland, one prototype, DX166, was completed in 1944, making its maiden flight in December but the Air Ministry cancelled an order for production aircraft in April 1945. Subsequently DX166 was destroyed by fire after an accident in January 1946. The other prototype, DX171, was not completed until 1947 and was registered as a civil transport, (G-AGVD). It was scrapped in 1951 without carrying a single passenger. Thus the unhappy story of the Shetland ended.

Meanwhile, Saunders-Roe remained convinced the flying boat had an important part to play in post war aviation, and that they should be in the forefront of development. In September 1944 an outline proposal by the design office at Beaumaris included a radical concept for a four engined machine powered by Rolls Royce Merlins in coupled pairs buried within the wing structure. The boat would have had a range of 3,000 miles at a cruising speed of 275 m.p.h. It was rejected by the Air Ministry.

Other designs, based on data obtained from the experimental flights of the ever-useful Shrimp, included a six engined transport with a 3,600 mile range and 317 m.p.h. maximum speed, and a design which utilised eight Bristol Centaurus engines buried in the wing to power a 250,000 lbs. aircraft at an estimated maximum speed of 330 m.p.h.

From these ideas grew the mighty Princess, a 200 seat flying boat powered by ten Bristol Proteus engines. But only three of the type were built and none entered service. They were cocooned at Calshot and scrapped in 1967.

Another radical design was the SR A/1 — a jet fighter flying boat. Powered by two Beryl 3,300 lbs. thrust engines, it had a maximum speed of 500 m.p.h. Much of the design and some manufacture of components took place at Beaumaris. Final assembly was at Cowes. Three prototypes were ordered in 1945 and the first flight took place in July 1947. However, as the 1940s drew to a close Air Ministry interest waned and the project was shelved in 1949.

Although Saunders-Roe clearly had a great deal of faith in flying boats the trend was against them. The Coronado, Shetland, and Princess were all failures and no satisfactory role, whether military or civil, could be found for them to occupy. However much the company wished it otherwise, the future lay with land based aircraft.

As far as Catalina conversion work at Friars was concerned the end of the war also meant the end of this task, though a marine tender and four moorings were retained for a short period in case of diversions by RAF flying boats. The possibility of using the site as a permanent flying boat base was considered briefly by the RAF immediately after the war but the idea was not pursued.

With the coming of peace Saunders-Roe decided to re-organise its widely dispersed factories, many of which were engaged on a variety of work now irrelevant to peacetime needs. Aircraft design and manufacture was to be concentrated at two centres, Cowes and Eastleigh.

This left something of a vacuum at the Beaumaris factory which the company attempted, successfully, to fill by switching to light engineering and construction of marine craft, principally MTBs (motor torpedo boats) and minesweepers. The MTBs were particularly powerful vessels capable of some very high speeds and were sold to a number of foreign navies, in addition to the Royal Navy.

Another important, if rather less exciting line of business during the immediate post war years was bus construction. Leyland chassis were delivered from their Midlands factory to Beaumaris, where bodies would then be fitted. Most of these vehicles were exported to South America. A major British customer was London Transport and a large number of their world famous red buses were built at Beaumaris in the 1940s.

In recent years the factory, after changes in both ownership and products, has experienced hard times and many redundancies have been imposed upon the workforce. At present contract work is being carried out for the Navy but the number of employees is very small. Some original wartime buildings remain in use however and the slipway with its tie down rings for flying boats is still extant.

Chapter 11

The Hills Take Their Toll
Flying Accidents in Snowdonia

During the war a great deal of flying training took place in North Wales, with aircraft operating day and night from local airfields such as Mona and Llandwrog in addition to bases in the Midlands, where a number of Operational Training Units (OTUs) were to be found.

There was intense flying activity by aircrew not fully trained and lacking experience, in an area which has the highest ground in England and Wales. Given these two factors the result was not difficult to predict — a multitude of accidents.

Throughout the war years a variety of aircraft, from single seat fighters to heavy bombers were destroyed and their crews killed after crashing into the mountains of Snowdonia. It is often said in aviation circles that aircraft and mountains do not mix and there is no doubt that the losses on this particular range of mountains bear out this statement.

Before 1940 high ground accidents were more or less non-existent in Gwynedd but from then onwards fatalities occurred during most months until 1945. A steady increase in the numbers of crashes was evident from early 1940, rising to a peak in 1942 and continuing at a high level until mid-1944 after which time a decline set in until the end of hostilities in 1945. Once the war ended so did the accidents.

If one wishes to analyse the causative factors behind these accidents, three are immediately apparent — statistical, technical failure and human error, with the last two often being inter-related in complex sequences which led so often to disaster.

As the number of flights increased so dramatically from pre-war days so did, statistically, the chances of an accident occurring. Generally, technical failures by themselves did not often cause accidents but mishandling or slowness in reacting to an emergency on the part of the crew following a malfunction frequently ended in an accident. As far as the Snowdonia crashes were concerned it was the third factor, human error, which predominated.

Frequent bad weather with continuous cloud cover, wartime 'blackout' conditions depriving pilots of visual clues at night, navigational errors, failure to keep a safety height of 5,000 feet or so when in a mountainous region, were the most common causes of accidents. In addition, many of the aircraft involved were low powered, such as the Anson, and once ensnared in a hilly area where updraughts and downdraughts of air were prevalent, these aircraft could be difficult, if not impossible, to control. Furthermore, not every pilot was aware of the dangers presented by strong air currents found in mountain areas. A few brief descriptions of some crashes will illustrate the foregoing points.

The crash of Blenheim L9309 on 8th April 1940, for instance. Whilst on a training flight from No.13 OTU, RAF Bicester to the Isle of Man this aircraft, in company with another Blenheim, encountered low cloud over Llangollen. The other aircraft climbed to a safe height of 4,500 feet but L9039 for some unknown reason continued at a dangerously low altitude until it struck the cloud — obscured rocky slopes of Craig yr Ysfa near Carnedd Llywelyn. The aircraft was at full power and in straight and level flight. Needless to say, the four men on board died instantly. A hillwalker found the wreckage on the following day.

Not every crash site was located quickly however. In the early days no properly co-ordinated rescue organisation existed and considerable lengths of time could elapse before a crashed aircraft was discovered, sometimes by chance. Spitfire X4239, for example, crashed near Ffestiniog in April 1942 after its American pilot became lost in thick cloud but the wreckage was not found for three weeks, an unimaginable state of affairs today when rescue teams can be at the scene of an accident almost within minutes.

Wellington DV800 suffered a similar fate when it crashed on a part of Carnedd Llywelyn known as Gilfach Felen in July 1942. The Wellington's wreckage and bodies of its five crew members lay on the mountainside for nine days before being discovered.

On Saturday afternoon, 21st July, a Bethesda quarryman, Robert Pritchard, was working in a potato field on his smallholding in Gerlan when he noticed that an area of ground on the mountainside above appeared to have been scorched. He did not investigate further, however. On Sunday morning he went a little way up the hillside but could not see anything. The weather was bad on Monday but on Tuesday, convinced that something was amiss, Robert Pritchard went higher up the hillside and with binoculars saw the wreckage of a crashed aircraft, which was in fact the missing Wellington. He reported what he had seen immediately to the Bethesda police.

A search party was quickly organised and went up to the crash site, to be confronted with a gruesome sight which shocked many in the party. Not only had the bodies of the crew suffered mutilation (this usually was the case in accidents of this nature) but parts had been eaten by birds of prey. The search party's report reveals the horror of the scene: "The rear turret was not badly damaged and inside was the body of the air gunner.

"Alongside this part of the plane were found two bodies, both badly mutilated by the crash and after by birds of prey, the intestines had been pulled out and flesh eaten away from the limbs. A short distance away from the rear turret another body was found, the remains however were just the backbone, the leg bone and lower part of the left foot, the birds had eaten all the loose flesh and parts of the body were missing."

"The clothing on the body of Sergeant. . .had been burnt, leaving several parts of the body uncovered and the birds had eaten some of the flesh, especially around the thighs."

The Wellington had taken off from RAF Lichfield, where it was based with No.27 OTU, on a four hour cross-country flight, first to Cannock in order to carry out practice bombing and then to the Isle of Man as a navigation exercise. From there it was to return to Lichfield, crossing the Welsh coast at Llandudno. Weather conditions were good in the Irish Sea but cloud hid the high ground of North Wales. It seems that the pilot entered this cloud, became lost, and then descended in order to try and ascertain his position, with fatal results. This flight was only the third cross-country exercise carried out by the crew of DV800.

The Great Orme at Llandudno was a convenient and obvious landmark on the North Wales coast, used as a crossing point by aircraft engaged on exercises in the Irish Sea. But the crossing point was changed to Rhyl following an accident in September 1942, when a Whitley pilot on a night navex (navigation exercise) apparently mistook Llandudno and the Conwy estuary for part of Merseyside. Believing himself to be well away from high ground the pilot turned to port, thereby heading directly for the Carneddau range of mountains. The Whitley crashed on Foel Fras, killing everyone on board.

Sometimes, when larger aircraft crashed, the loss of life could be considerable. A Dakota which flew into Moel Morfydd, 3½ miles north west of Llangollen during August 1942 had twelve men on board, ten of whom were killed and the other two seriously injured. Twelve months later a B-17 from the 303rd Bombardment Group, USAF Molesworth, crashed on the north west face of Arenig Fawr, killing ten men. A memorial plaque has subsequently been erected on the mountain. Another B-17 crashed in June 1945 near Barmouth, killing twenty.

Most high ground accidents had but one fatal result but sometimes there were survivors to tell the tale. One such accident, with an interesting sequel, took place on 14th April 1941 and is here described in some detail. The aircraft was a German bomber which crashed on the slopes of Llwytmor mountain above the village of Aber.

This particular aircraft, a Heinkel III, code letters IT+EL, had taken off from its base at Nantes in northern France late in the evening of the 13th with the objective of attacking the aircraft carrier *Victorious*, which was at Barrow-in-Furness.

Pilot and captain of the Heinkel was Leutnant Lothar Horras, with a crew of three — Navigator/Observer, Feltwebel Bruno Perzanowski, who was also the bomb aimer (and a fanatical Nazi!), the Flight Engineer was Gefreiter Josef Brünninghausen and Gefreiter Kurt Schlender was the Wireless Operator. Their unit was the 3rd Staffel of K.G.28, whose main task was the mining of British coastal waters and ports.

After taking off the aircraft crossed the French coast near St.Malo and then took an over-water route; the English Channel, St.George's Channel and the Irish Sea before turning east for the English coast and Barrow.

Once over the port, Horras and his crew experienced no difficulty in locating the Vickers Armstrong shipyard, where the *Victorious* was docked, according to intelligence reports resulting from a reconnaissance flight carried out the previous day. But the aircraft carrier was not there. Wisely, she had been moved to another dock as a precautionary measure following the alert caused by the previous day's flight.

Unable to locate their prime target the Heinkel's disappointed crew decided to drop their bombs on some harbour installations. However, just as the bombs were dropping one of the crew spotted the *Victorious* in a different area of the port to that which had been expected, but of course it was far too late to modify their plan.

To make matters worse the crew's disappointment soon turned to consternation when ground defences sprang into action and began to direct very heavy, and accurate, anti-aircraft gunfire at the Heinkel. Explosions from bursting shells shook the aircraft violently and flak caused damage to the radio, compass, auto-pilot and flight instruments.

Lt.Horras decided it was time to withdraw. . ."We pulled out because we had been hit and I was not sure whether it was just the cockpit or whether the engines, also, had been hit."

"But the engines were OK and so we flew on, at low level, in the direction of Anglesey." The intention was to reach home by skirting the British coast though the risk of running out of fuel had to be considered. A direct flight across England would have eliminated this problem and saved much time but the chance of being intercepted by enemy fighters was too great.

"We stayed low, some 150-300 feet, trying to get close to the coast but since our main compass was out of action and the weather continued to be quite bad, with showers and often zero visibility, I decided to gain height since I was afraid of crashing, even on the coast of Anglesey."

"As the Heinkel was beginning to climb I realised she was climbing fast, much faster than normal. It was obvious we were in an updraught, then Brünninghausen, my flight engineer, called out, 'Mountains, Lieutenant!' ". They were in Snowdonia.

"After that we got into an equally strong downdraught and despite both engines running at full throttle it took me some time before the aircraft started to climb again. Just when I thought I had overcome the problem it suddenly went completely dark in front of me. I pulled the steering column right back with both hands and then everything went black. . ."

"When I came round I found myself lying on the ground looking at flames. It was my aircraft burning. I couldn't get up. I saw Perzanowski coming towards me and it was he who pulled me up. He had been injured but had got his brains working more quickly than I had. I was still dazed."

"We stood there for a moment, then suddenly he threw me to the ground again because the ammunition was now exploding. After the fire died down we went up to the wreckage and found Brünninghausen. But Schlender was missing and we could not find him. Then we saw a man coming up the slope towards us. We thought he was an English soldier but it was Schlender, who had been thrown well clear of the wreckage after we crashed."

"He then helped me put dressings on my wounds. It was light by now but we couldn't see anything much because of mist. I said, 'We'll have to try and find someone. I suppose nobody knows we are here.' There seemed to be a path nearby so I said to Schlender, 'Try and go down that path.' He went, but I didn't wait for him to return. I said, 'Come on Perzanowski, let's try and go down the same path'."

"We went down this path, crossed a stream and finally, after being met by policemen and soldiers we ended up in a cottage, where we were looked after with the most touching care."

Kurt Schlender takes up the story from his viewpoint: "Aboard the Heinkel everything was quiet. I had an altitude meter and it indicated we had reached some three thousand feet. One of the crew said, 'Did you notice anything just now, what was it?' Yes, I had noticed something whizzing past and that must have been a mountain peak we had just skimmed."

"We were flying in the clouds, visibility was zero. Then there was a bang, followed by total silence. The engine noise had stopped. My first thought was that we had been caught by a barrage balloon! The perspex dome I had been sitting under had gone. I grabbed my parachute and was just about to jump out when I realised that we were on the ground."

The wide sweep of Hell's Mouth Bay

Former site of RAF Hell's Mouth

631 Squadron pilots outside the officer's mess at Llanbedr
(Photo: J. Law)

Vultee Vengeance Target Tug of 631 Squadron, Llanbedr
(Photo: J. Law)

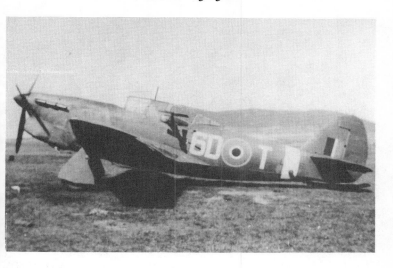

Hawker Henley Target Tower at RAF Tywyn (Photo: A. B. Pudney)

631 Squadron, with Hurricane at Tywyn. The shell cases on the table show the various type of ammunition fired by the Army at targets towed by 631 Squadron (Photo: A. B. Pudney, 4th left, front row)

The Duke of Kent on a visit to the Hunting Aviation Factory at Dinorwig in May 1942. On the Duke's right is Sir Percy Hunting and behind them stands Sir Goronwy Owen, M.P. On the Duke's left is W. A. Summers, the Works Manager (Photo: W. A. Summers)

Lloyd George, centre, visits the Hunting Aviation Factory at Dinorwig (Photo: W. A. Summers)

*Henry Knowler, (facing camera), C.1949. Behind him
is the huge bulk of the Saunders-Roe Princess,
the largest flying boat in the world when it first flew in 1952
(Photo: British Hovercraft Corporation)*

Catalinas in the Menai Straits (Photo: Winifred Brown)

Catalina MK.IVa JX246 on the slipway
(Photo: British Hovercraft Corporation)

Two Catalinas in the snow (Photo: British Hovercraft Corporation)

Auster VP-FAC in the Menai Straits (Photo: Les Leetham Collection)

Auster Floatplane Prototype TJ207 at Beaumaris, 1944/45.
Test pilot Les Ash can be seen dressed in white overalls
(Photo: Auster Pilot Club)

An aerial photograph of the former Saunders-Roe factory at Beaumaris in 1987

Caernarfon photographed from a Short Sunderland in August 1944

Kurt Schlender in 1941

Horras and Schlender inspect a piece of wreckage from their Heinkel on Llwytmor mountain (Photo: D. Roberts)

A Heinkel HEIII similar to that which crashed on Llwytmor in April 1941 (Photo: Imperial War Museum)

Ace Schultz (left), pilot of 'Bachelor's Baby'
on his return to the crash site in 1978

Crash site of 'Bachelor's Baby', with memorial plaque and cross,
near Moelfre mountain above the village of Llanfairfechan.
No vegetation has grown on the site since the crash

Crash of Spitfire L1034 at Beaumaris in March 1941

34 M.U. Salvage Gang at work on the wreckage of a B-17 which crashed near Barmouth in June 1945 (Photo: D. Roberts)

*Merlin engine from Mosquito W4088
which crashed on Mynydd Mawr in November 1944*

*Wing section from Douglas Boston Z2186
which crashed on Carnedd Dafydd in 1942*

*Anson N5371 of Llandwrog after crashing on Foel Fras in August 1943
(Photo: D. Roberts)*

*Bristol Perseus engine from Blackburn Botha L6202
which crashed on Llwytmor in 1943*

*Mercury Radial engine from Blenheim L9039
lies at the foot of Craig-yr-Ysfa*

*Plaque erected at Nant Peris in memory of the crew of
Martin Marauder 44-68072*

Memorial plaque on the summit of Arenig Fawr, near Bala, erected in memory of the crew of B-17 42-3124 which crashed here in August 1943 with no survivors

An unusual memorial to dead airmen — a Merlin engine from Mosquito LR412, which crashed on Aran Fawddwy Mountain in February 1944, now embedded in concrete on a stone plinth at the entrance to Esgair Fawr Farm at the foot of the mountain

"There was rocky terrain all around me. I took cover behind a huge rock because, by now, the ammunition was exploding. I thought I was the only survivor and towards dawn, when the fire had subsided somewhat, I went over to the crash scene and there the pilot and observer were sitting."

"Then we took stock: Horras had all but lost two fingers — they were dangling from a tendon. What was to be done? We all three debated and decided there was no other way but to cut off the fingers. So I took them off, put a bandage on, and strapped everything down. All was to be well, the injury healed properly and there was no blood poisoning even."

"The other two were immobilised and in shock so I suggested that I should go down and get help. They didn't want to be left alone but I said, 'It's got to be done. Nobody is going to find us up here.' So I went down, and some two hundred yards behind the aircraft I found the body of Brünninghausen.

"The fact that anyone got out alive at all is probably due to the fact that the aircraft was climbing at the time, its angle of climb was roughly equal to the mountain slope — a kind of uphill belly landing."

"By a stroke of luck I found the right way down. After a while I saw a small river and a cottage with smoke rising from the chimney. I waded through the river after casting my pistol away in order not to appear too aggressive, and I then knocked on the door. It was opened by an elderly lady whom I told in broken English that I was a German airman."

The cottage was, in fact, Cydcoed, in the Aber Valley about one mile from the village of Aber, between Bangor and Llanfairfechan. The 'elderly lady' was Mrs Marion Baxter. She was preparing breakfast at the time (7.20 a.m.) and thought it was the postman knocking at the door. Instead, to her astonishment she found a rather bedraggled looking man dressed in a German uniform saying that he was a crashed airman. Mrs Baxter quickly recovered her composure and invited him in for a cup of tea!

Then, whilst she went to telephone the authorities her husband took charge of Schlender. Presently the police and Home Guard arrived. Schlender was then interrogated by an officer: "He asked me whether I was feeling strong enough to climb back up to the crash since my comrades were still up there. I said yes, so a policeman lent me his raincoat — it was raining — and we went up again. After a short while we met Horras and Perzanowski hobbling towards us, supporting one another."

The body of the flight engineer had still to be recovered and so a party, including Schlender, continued up to the crash site. It was still misty but the wreckage was easily located because of the smell of smoke.

From Aber the survivors were taken to hospital at Bangor, where their injuries were treated. They were subsequently incarcerated as prisoners of war, ending up in Canadian POW camps.

After the war Horras and Schlender were repatriated to Germany but not Perzanowski. Reference has already been made to his fanatical adherence to Nazi ideology and it was this extreme zeal which led to his tragic end. During the time he spent as a prisoner of war in Canada he, along with three other diehard Nazis, murdered a fellow German whom they accused of being a Communist. For this crime all four were executed in December 1946.

Nearly half a century after the Heinkel's crash Harlech Television decided, in 1989, to make a film about wartime crashes in Snowdonia. They contacted Horras and Schlender, who were flown to Britain, where they stayed as guests of Harlech TV. During the long hot summer of that year they were taken by helicopter to the crash site of their Heinkel, where filming took place. It was an emotional moment for them both to be re-united on the mountainside where they had last stood, as crash survivors, back in 1941.

Another similar type of crash, with survivors returning many years later, took place on high ground between the villages of Llanfairfechan and Penmaenmawr.

On this occasion the aircraft was American, a B-24 which formed part of the huge influx of US Eighth Air Force aircraft into Britain from mid 1943 onwards. Like many others before, this particular B-24, serial 42-99991 and named "Bachelor's Baby", had flown into RAF Valley after a long haul from the United States. Its final destination was the Eighth Air Force base at Watton in East Anglia.

After landing at Valley on 3rd January 1944 bad weather kept the B-24 grounded until the 6th when a B-17 arrived to act as 'shepherd'. By then six other B-24s had also landed at Valley. They successfully took off and followed the B-17 but "Bachelor's Baby", who was last, received orders whilst it was taxying to return and pick up a crew member from another aircraft, who had missed his flight. Before "Bachelor's Baby" could once again prepare for take off the weather worsened and the aircraft had to remain where it was. On the 7th weather conditions were still bad — low cloud, fog patches and intermittent rain. This did not deter the 'shepherd' B-17 which arrived late in the morning to lead the B-24 on the last leg of its journey.

In the event, it was literally the last leg. Just before 2.00 p.m. the two aircraft were airborne, flying under extensive low cloud. In command of the B-24 was 2nd Lt. A. Shultz, with ten other men on board. Schultz was maintaining visual contact with the B-17 as they approached the eastern end of the Menai Straits. Then the B-17 pilot radioed that he was climbing and setting a course.

Unfortunately Schultz could not maintain contact and lost the B-17 as it disappeared into cloud. Worryingly, all he could see ahead was a range of hills partly obscured by the cloud. He then radioed the escort pilot to inform him that he had lost contact, to which the other pilot replied by telling him to maintain his course. Schultz was not flying a course at all and radioed again to say that he was preparing to climb up through the cloud layer and re-establish contact in the clear air above.

He then applied more power to the B-24 and initiated a climbing turn. However, as the aircraft climbed into the all enveloping cloud it was flying at a dangerously low height as it rapidly approached the coastal village of Llanfairfechan and the hills rising beyond. The danger became apparent to all on board a few seconds later when the B-24 touched the roof ridge of a house before taking the tops off a line of trees. It then headed towards the cloud obscured mountains behind Llanfairfechan.

Disaster was but a few seconds away, as graphically described by Edward Doylerush in *No Landing Place*, (Midland Counties Publications 1985):-

> "Schultz had slammed the throttles into the stops to gain height, heading for a lighter 'V' in the mist that might take them to safety. Boyer (the bomb aimer), in the navigator's compartment could see the grass coming up, but not having a mike on, could not tell the pilot. He braced himself against the command deck thinking of his mother and hoping the end would be instantaneous. A second later they hit, just below a rocky knoll known locally as Mynydd Bach, a ridge coming away from Penmaenmawr mountain."

But the aircraft was not totally out of control. It still continued to fly (just) as Schultz struggled with the wheel:

> "Number four propeller and the fuselage had hit the ground simultaneously. The impact dragged off the bomb bay doors so that all the baggage and spares were strewn along the flight path for some 150 yards. As Schultz regained control the aircraft took off again over a plateau for another 600 yards, slowly losing height, and made contact this time on wild and boggy terrain. Schultz hit his head on the windscreen demister almost knocking him out. Mud and stones shot into the air as the Liberator ploughed up a slope, finally slewing round and coming to a halt at the foot of Moelfre mountain".

Three of the eleven men on board were killed and the others all suffered some degree of injury. Two later died as a result of their injuries.

In the B-24's bomb bay, alongside quantities of spare parts and personal luggage, some contraband had been stowed, including cigarettes, chocolates etc. in addition to silk and leather goods from Morocco.

Thirty years later, in the 1970s, one of Llanfairfechan's residents, Mr Jack Bohanna, who had been much affected by the crash, decided to trace the surviving crew. Eventually he succeeded in contacting Schultz who was living in Tampa, Florida. After his accident he never flew again but he had remained in the Air Force, retiring in 1962 with the rank of Major. In 1977 he returned to Llanfairfechan as a guest of Jack Bohanna and during his stay revisited the crash site. Since then he has returned a number of times. During his 1980 visit he had an unusual duty to perform.

Mr Bohanna and his friends wished to erect a memorial at the bottom of Moelfre mountain, and so, in March an American Air Force helicopter airlifted a slate plaque, suitably inscribed, together with about twenty passengers to the site. After a short service conducted by the Rector of Llanfairfechan, the memorial plaque was unveiled by Major Schultz. In September 1984 another survivor, Julian Ertz, who was the B-24's navigator, paid a visit to Llanfairfechan. His back was broken in the accident and he still suffers from the effects.

Unlikely though it seems wartime accidents have occurred at exactly the same spot, twice over. In October 1943 Anson LT184 crashed on the slopes of Mynydd Perfedd near Bethesda after being caught in bad weather whilst on a cross-country training flight. All the crew died. At the subsequent inquiry the pilot was blamed for failing to maintain height and not abandoning the exercise when he flew into bad weather. The conclusion, as in so many cases, was pilot error. Then, in June 1944 Anson LT116, on a night flying exercise from Llandwrog crashed at precisely the same part of Mynydd Perfedd, killing all five crew members.

Sometimes the time interval between two unrelated accidents in the mountains was hours only. For instance, RAF Penrhos lost two aircraft in one afternoon during November 1942. At midday on the 20th Henley L3334 took off on a training flight but shortly after entering low cloud in the Cwm Silyn area the 26 year old pilot became lost. Unfortunately he flew into cliffs above Cwm Silyn, with the usual fatal consequence.

Two hours later another Penrhos aircraft, Anson N4981, took off with five crew on board to carry out navigation exercises. Like the Henley it encountered thick cloud and began to wander off course.

By then a search party from Llandwrog, led by the SMO, Flight

Lieutenant G. Graham had set out for Cwm Silyn hoping to locate the crashed Henley despite bad weather.

Graham, with commendable humanitarian initiative, had been the originator of a rescue party using volunteers drawn from Llandwrog's SSQ, which went into the mountains in search of survivors from crashed aircraft. The Llandwrog mountain rescue team, once its value had been established, became the model for other teams operating a similar 'service' in high ground areas of Britain such as the Lake District and Scotland. From these beginnings in North Wales has grown the present day highly trained RAF Mountain Rescue organisation.

Back in Cwm Silyn the search party failed to find the Henley because thick mist restricted visibility to a few yards. Had they been able to locate the crash site they could have done little to help the pilot as the aircraft had impacted on cliffs inaccessible without climbing skills, which the Llandwrog party at that time, did not possess. When the wreckage was eventually discovered, recovering the pilot's body proved extremely difficult and the assistance of quarrymen from the Nantlle Slate Quarry nearby was sought. Experienced in the use of ropes, they were able to negotiate the steep rock face of the cliffs and reach a gully where the dead pilot lay.

Meanwhile, the Anson was seen flying over Nant-y-Betws at about 2.30 p.m. but seconds later it crashed into the cloud-obscured southern side of Moel Eilio, five miles from the earlier crash of that afternoon. Local residents in the valley heard the crash and searched the hillside for wreckage, which they found within an hour. Four of the crew were dead but one man was alive though injured. Sadly he died a few hours later from exposure and shock, before proper medical assistance was available. The person who could possible have saved the man's life, Flight Lieutenant Graham, was in Cwm Silyn leading the fruitless search for the Henley.

Two months later, one of Llandwrog's Ansons failed to return from a cross country flight on 14th January 1943. On the following day, with a cloud base of 2,000 feet, a limited air search revealed nothing, but in the afternoon the Anson's pilot, Pilot Officer Archer, stumbled into a farmhouse near Talybont in the Conwy valley. He was exhausted and in a confused state of mind. When the rescue party arrived from Llandwrog, led as usual by Fl.Lt. Graham (awarded the MBE that month in recognition of his efforts in setting up a rescue organisation in Snowdonia) they found Pilot Officer Archer still confused and incapable of providing details about the crash. All he could remember was crashing somewhere in the mountains, leaving the aircraft with three other crew members still alive in it, climbing up a hillside and then down scree, past two lakes.

Following a lengthy and somewhat disorganised search, hampered by bad weather, the Anson was eventually located in a gully above Llyn Dulyn. One man was alive, suffering from a broken arm and jaw but the other two had succumbed to the effects of shock and exposure and were dead.

The unsatisfactory outcome of this rescue, coming so soon after the Moel Eilio crash, troubled Fl.Lt. Graham. In both cases men had died because the rescue organisation was not as efficient as it could be. Lack of resources and the resultant need to improvise was costing lives, in Graham's view. The only way to improve efficiency, he thought, was the provision of proper equipment, transport, and the training of team members in mountaincraft.

After the higher echelons of the RAF and Air Ministry had been convinced of the usefulness of mountain rescue teams, transport capable of traversing rough ground, radio sets, mountaineering equipment, ropes, boots, clothing etc. were forthcoming. Equally important was the teaching of climbing and hillwalking skills to the team members, turning them into technically competent mountaineers able to negotiate any kind of terrain in all weathers with confidence and safety. By the end of 1943, a year when the accident rate was high, thirty three survivors had been rescued from twenty two crashes — positive proof of the team's value.

Besides Fl.Lt. Graham (posted overseas in January 1944) others within the Air Ministry were taking positive steps to reduce deaths from flying accidents in mountain areas. The Directorate of Aircraft Safety had become so concerned at the number of accidents in Snowdonia (ten during the latter half of 1942, killing forty men and injuring eight) and other mountain areas of Britain that it decided action was needed to reduce losses.

In July 1943 the Directorate introduced an experimental scheme known as Operation Granite for a two month trial period in the Peak District. Under this scheme ROC posts would fire red flares whenever an aircraft was plotted approaching under 'bad weather' conditions, defined for the purpose of the trial as cloud down to the 1,000 foot contour. Flares would continue to be fired until the plot faded or turned on to a track away from high ground. Pilots were instructed to fly a reciprocal course immediately they saw a flare burning. After an extension of the two month trial to September 1943, Granite was judged successful and put into operation in other areas including North Wales, the Pennines, the Lake District and parts of the Scottish Highlands. Before the scheme's commencement date, 21st February 1944, the Air Ministry came up with

Augmented Granite, which gave audio as well as visual warning to a pilot that he was approaching high ground. A simple beacon transmitter placed at some suitable point in the mountains emitted signals which could be picked up by approaching aircraft. Servicing was minimal, consisting of nothing more than changing batteries every two months.

On 4th January 1944 Flight Lieutenant Simkins, a signals officer from RAE Farnborough arrived at Llandwrog with two transmitters. He was led by the station's Mountain Rescue Team to the summit of Foel Fras where one transmitter was placed. The second was positioned in Cwm Silyn.

Pilots instructions were to take immediate action as seemed reasonable in the circumstances, normally to go on a reciprocal without delay if below cloud or to climb if in cloud — and hope for the best!

On at least three occasions Granite proved effective in preventing aircraft from flying into high ground in North Wales, and there may well have been other times of course. Llanegryn ROC post in the extreme south of Gwynedd operated the system on 29th March 1944 when an aircraft came in from the west, heading towards high ground. After flares had been fired, the aircraft rapidly made height, eventually being plotted out of the area at 7,000 feet, well above safety height.

The Penygroes post also had an opportunity to operate Granite on 3rd June 1944 when an Anson was plotted heading towards the mountains at less than 1,000 feet height. Luckily its pilot saw the red flares and took a reciprocal course. In October Wrexham ROC saved an Oxford from disaster in similar circumstances. The pilot later informed those responsible how pleased he was to receive their warning as he thought he had been much further east, flying over lower ground.

As 1944 progressed high ground accidents were becoming fewer in North Wales but not primarily as a result of Granite. The relentless pressure of training, so characteristic of previous years, was beginning to ease and as flying decreased so did accidents.

By 1945 the accident rate was dropping rapidly with the last two wartime crashes occurring on 17th May, when a Mustang crashed on Aran Fawddwy near Bala, and on 8th June when an American B-17 flew into high ground near Barmouth, killing all twenty people on board. During the war some fifty high ground accidents in Gwynedd killed nearly two hundred aircrew in addition to injuring many others. Such was the toll of the hills.

The reader might well ask what happened to the wreckage of all those crashed aircraft? Was it left on the hillside or was it all carefully removed, right down to the smallest piece of debris? The answer usually lay somewhere in between the two possibilities.

To deal with this problem the Air Ministry established a number of Maintenance Units solely responsible for the salvage of crashed aircraft — No.34 MU based at Shrewsbury had responsibility for North Wales. The priorities involved in salvage operations were twofold. Firstly, to recover any serviceable items and material for further use and secondly, to burn or bury remaining wreckage in order to eliminiate the risk of false reports of crashes by overflying aircraft.

Many forms of transport, from horses to tractors, were used to bring wreckage down from the hillsides but often material had to be manhandled over rough and difficult mountain terrain by the men themselves. Today helicopters would be used, but this most versatile machine was not available then to ease the burden of salvage teams in their rather unpleasant and thankless task. They often complained that they were the forgotten men of the RAF.

In Snowdonia few of the crash sites were totally cleared of wreckage, with many items such as engines and propellers being left as they were, mangled and torn, on the ground. Much of this wreckage can still be seen today on the slopes of numerous mountains and valleys in the region.

However, in the last few years interest in wartime crashes has grown considerably and many items of wreckage have disappeared, either plundered by souvenir hunters or taken legitimately, with Ministry of Defence approval, for display in aviation museums etc.

Much research has been carried out on these crashes and a wealth of information is available on the subject. For an interesting account of crashes in Snowdonia the reader is advised to consult the previously mentioned publication *No Landing Place* by Edward Doylerush. This book's principal interest lies in the first-hand accounts of accidents provided by survivors.

A number of memorial plaques have been erected at crash sites such as Aran Fawddwy and Moelfre Mountain, for instance. They serve as a fitting and permanent reminder, not only of the men who died there, but also of all the others who lost their lives on the bleak and lonely hillsides of Snowdonia.

Conclusion

By the autumn of 1945 all of Gwynedd's airfields had either closed or were operating at a much reduced level. The intense activity of the war years had melted away with even more rapidity than it had begun. Aviation had come to Gwynedd because of the war and now that victory had been achieved one of its consequences was to render redundant all RAF aircrew training carried out within the area. It was a time of rapid wind down.

At Valley the Americans had departed, leaving behind only one small RAF unit, 1528 RAT Flight, still using the airfield. Mona, after disbandment of the flying unit, went on a Care and Maintenance basis and Bodorgan had closed to all traffic by August. Later, after use of its buildings to house Italian POWs it reverted to agriculture thus ensuring there would be no further flying from this location.

At Llandwrog and Penrhos flying ended in June following which Aircrew Holding Units took over the domestic accommodation for a few months. Large numbers of aircrew stayed here for short periods before being sent to other units or returning to civilian life. Hell's Mouth was closed completely as an airfield but RAF plans to extend the bombing range were thwarted by public opposition and the land reverted to agriculture in 1947. Tywyn closed in July and was eventually taken over by the army. Its closest neighbour, Llanbedr, remained open however, though only as a base for 631 Squadron, engaged on army co-operation and the unglamorous task of target towing. At Beaumaris, where Saunders-Roe had their factory, flying activity had come to an end in September.

Decisions regarding the long term future lay with the Post War Airfields Requirements Committee of the Air Ministry but for the immediate future there was little to do except maintain the C. & M. basis of the airfields and ensure the removal of aircraft to various MUs for final disposal.

By the early 1950s, after a period of uncertainty, the situation had become clearer. Valley, following use in the late 1940s by No.2 (Pilots) Refresher Flying Unit, was to become an advanced flying school for jet pilots with Mona used as a relief landing ground and Llanbedr was to be an outstation of RAE Farnborough, where research into pilotless target drones was to be carried out. The RAF had no further interest in the remaining five airfields.

However, use by civilian light aircraft has continued in some form or another at two — Penrhos and Llandwrog, now renamed Caernarfon Airport. In addition Mona became the home of a civilian flying club in the mid 1970s. Thus of the eight wartime airfields, it is from three only, Bodorgan, Tywyn and Hell's Mouth, that aviation has disappeared completely in the post-war period.

Use of local airspace by the military has not changed, in essence, since the war. The region is still primarily a training area with the difference that aircraft now are jets and they fly much faster than was previously the case, especially in the mountainous parts of North Wales. It is a pattern that has been maintained for some fifty years now and seems set to continue into the next century. Such has been the legacy of the war.

But if the type of flying has not changed what of the airfields themselves? What would a young airman of the 1940s find today if he returned? He would find that six of the eight have kept their original layout, though two, Valley and Llanbedr, have been developed into modern airfields with much new building having taken place, particularly in recent years. Only at two, Hell's Mouth and Tywyn have all physical traces of their existence been obliterated. As for the others, Mona, Bodorgan, Llandwrog and Penrhos, runways have been closed, hangars and buildings demolished or fallen into ruin but nevertheless, despite the dereliction much remains to remind one of their original purpose.

At Bodorgan, for instance, the landing ground has not been re-hedged and many of the buildings continue in everyday use whilst at Penrhos most of the domestic site still stands, being the home of Polish ex-servicemen.

Indeed, there is a great deal to delight the present day aviation enthusiast bent on exploring these airfield sites, and there is an added bonus too. All are to be found in scenically attractive areas, never far from mountain or sea. Who could fail to notice the surroundings of Llandwrog for example, with the mountains of Snowdonia on one side and the waters of Caernarfon Bay on the other? If the visitor wanted to recapture something of the past there is no better place than Bodorgan with its many RAF utility buildings set in a rural scene which has changed little since 1945.

Or the visitor could stand on the headland half a mile from Beaumaris and look out upon a wide, beautiful bay with the site of the old Saunders-Roe factory on his left, still with its slipway and tie-down rings for Catalina flying boats. It is easy to imagine what it must have been like half a century before, with elegant looking Catalinas riding at their moorings in the bay.

The same can be said of all the other sites. There is plenty of airfield architecture and physical evidence of the past for the aviation enthusiast to explore and enjoy.

Since the 1940s aviation has become firmly established in the region and has undergone much development and will undoubtedly continue to do so in the years to come but whatever the future holds, one can state with confidence that it will not bear comparison with the unique period of the war years.

It is no exaggeration to say that the second World War represents an epoch for aviation in Gwynedd and furthermore, it is highly unlikely that we shall ever see anything like it again.

Abbreviations

AACU	— Anti Aircraft Co-operation Unit
ACHU	— Aircrew Holding Unit
AFU	— Advanced Flying Unit
AGS	— Air Gunnery School
AOA	— Air Officer Administration
AOC	— Air Officer Commanding
AOS	— Air Observers School
ASR	— Air Sea Rescue
ASV	— Air to Surface Vessel (Radar)
ATA	— Air Transport Auxiliary
BAT	— Blind Approach Training (Flight)
BGS	— Bombing and Gunnery School
C & M	— Care and Maintenance
DPCA	— Directorate of Production, Canadian and American (Aircraft)
DTD	— Directorate, Technical Development
FC	— Fighter Command
FTC	— Flying Training Command
FTS	— Flying Training School
GCI	— Ground Controlled Interception
IR	— Infra Red
ITW	— Initial Training Wing
LRASV	— Long Range Air to Surface Vessel (Radar)
MAP	— Ministry of Aircraft Production
MAEE	— Marine Aircraft Experimental Establishment
MU	— Maintenance Unit
OAFU	— Observers Advanced Flying Unit
OTU	— Operational Training Unit
PAFU	— Pilots Advanced Flying Unit
RAE	— Royal Aircraft Establishment
RAT	— Radio Aids Training (Flight)
RATOG	— Rocket Assisted Take Off Gear
RCAF	— Royal Canadian Air Force
RFC	— Royal Flying Corps
RFU	— Refresher Flying Unit
RLG	— Relief Landing Ground
RNAS	— Royal Naval Air Service
ROC	— Royal Observer Corps
R/T	— Radio Telephony
SASO	— Senior Air Staff Officer
SFTS	— Service Flying Training School
SHQ	— Station Headquarters
SLG	— Satellite Landing Ground
SMO	— Station Medical Officer

SSQ	— Station Sick Quarters
TFU	— Telecommunications Flying Unit
USAAF	— United States Army Air Force

References

RAF Valley
Military Aviation Review, June/July 1981
PRO — Air 28/874 Valley Operations Record Book, WWII
Air 16/583 Valley Admin. Matters
Squadron Operations Record Books: 68, 131, 157, 219, 350, 406, 456, and 615 Squadron
Air 20/4352 — Col. Turner's Department
Air 20/4353 — Col. Turner's Department historical review
Roll No.A0169 — 16mm microfilm — history of 1407th base unit, Valley.
US Air Force Historical Research Center, Maxwell Air Force Base, Alabama, U.S.A.

RAF Mona
PRO — Air 28/560 Operations Record Book
Air 29/590 No.3 AGS Operations Record Book
Air 29/547 No.8(0) AFU Operations Record Book

RAF Bodorgan
PRO — Air 28/88 Operations Record Book
Air 29/880 No.1606 Flight
Air 29/955 No.70 Group Leaders School
Bodorgan Estate papers 1939-45

RAF Llandwrog
Aeromilitaria No.4/76 and 1/77
RAF Llandwrog 1940-45, by Wing Commander D. Annand, published by the author, 1986
PRO — Air 29/597 No.9 AGS
PRO — Air 29/2017 31 MU Llanberis

RAF Penrhos
Aeromilitaria No.4/76 and 1/77
RAF Penrhos 1937-45 by Wing Commander D. Annand, published by the author, 1983
PRO — Air 20/4352
PRO — Air 29/547

RAF Llanbedr	PRO — Air 28/494 Operations Record Book *History of Llanbedr*, by Wing Commander D. Annand, published by the author, 1983
RAF Towyn	PRO — Air 29/880 *RAF Tywyn 1940-45* by Wing Commander D. Annand, published by the author 1983
Saunders Roe Ltd.	Unpublished paper "Conversion of American Aircraft by Saunders Roe Ltd. during the War of 1939-45", April 1948 — R. Aero. Soc. Library. *No Distress Signals*, Winifred Brown, London 1952, Peter Davies Ltd.
Accidents	Snowdonia Aviation Historical Society, guide to warplane wrecks. *No Landing Place*, E. Doylerush, Midland Counties Publications 1985 PRO — Air 20/5338 Operation Granite

References — General

Action Stations, D. J. Smith, Patrick Stephens Ltd., Cambridge 1981
Daily Post, November 14th-17th 1966 — "Attack from the West", I. W. Jones
PRO —   Air 2/5225 No.9 Group Organisation
              Air 2/4573 Organisation and Foundation of No.9 Group
              Avia 15/900 Radar
Llangefni Record Office, WDAG/1 & 2
Caernarfon Record Office DQ1783 — Use of Dinorwig Quarry by Necaco Ltd.
Royal Observer Corps papers — UCNW archives.
The Air War Over Gwynedd — Snowdonia Aviation Historical Group.

Named Lysander, "Aurora", T1526 of 1486 Gunnery Flight, Valley, in 1942 (photo: D. Pritchard)

Beaufighters of 406 (RCAF) Squadron at Valley in 1943 (photo: D. Pritchard)

Bristol Beaufighter, coded RX-E, of 456 (RAAF) Squadron at Valley in December 1942 (photo: B. Richardson via Jack Ross)

Aerial photograph of Mona on 31 May, 1960 (photo Crown Copyright)

The well known Avro Anson MK.I — a type used for training aircrew at many airfields, including Mona, Llandwrog and Penrhos (photo: Imperial War Museum)

The de Havilland Queen Bee, a type used extensively at Bodorgan (photo: Imperial War Museum)

*An Armstrong-Whitworth Whitley similar to those at Llandwrog
(photo: Imperial War Museum)*

Lysander Target Tug releasing drogue (photo: Imperial War Museum)

Hawker Demon K8197 with Fairey Battles at Penrhos (photo: RAF Museum)

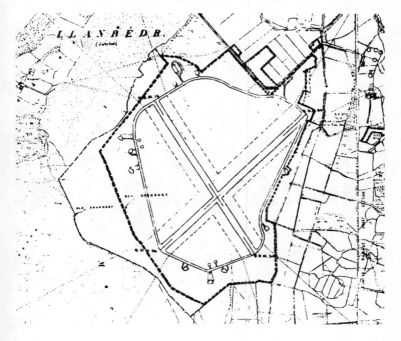

Aerial photograph of Tywyn, 4 May, 1946 (photo: Crown Copyright)

The Saro A.37 "Shrimp" used extensively at Beaumaris as a research vehicle for flying boat development (photo: Imperial War Museuem)

Spitfire Floatplane in the grounds of 'Friars'
(photo: British Hovercraft Corporation)

An example of a Junkers JU88 similar to that which crashed at Clywedog in 1940.
The JU88 was one of the most frequently seen of German Aircraft types in North Wales
(photo: Imperial War Museum)

*Lothar Horras at the controls of a Heinkel Bomber,
with Flight Engineer Josef Brünninghausen behind (photo: HTV)*

Index